Witness Lee

Living Stream Ministry
Anaheim, CA • www.lsm.org

© 1980 Living Stream Ministry

All rights reserved. No part of this work may be reproduced or transmitted in any form or by any means—graphic, electronic, or mechanical, including photocopying, recording, or information storage and retrieval systems—without written permission from the publisher.

First Edition, June 1989.

ISBN 0-87083-446-0 (hardcover)
ISBN 0-87083-447-9 (softcover)

Published by

Living Stream Ministry
2431 W. La Palma Ave., Anaheim, CA 92801 U.S.A.
P. O. Box 2121, Anaheim, CA 92814 U.S.A.

Printed in the United States of America
05 06 07 08 09 10 / 10 9 8 7 6 5 4 3 2

CONTENTS

Title	Page
Preface	v
1 Christ in Ascension	1
2 Christ in God's Administration	9
3 Christ in the Building Up of the Church	17
4 Christ in the Growth and Function of the Believers for the Building Up of the Body	25
5 Our Corresponding to Christ's Heavenly Ministry under His Headship	33
6 How We Hold the Head and Grow into Him in All Things	41
7 The Heavenly Priesthood of Christ	49
8 Christ's Execution of the New Testament	57
9 The More Excellent Ministry of Christ in the True Tabernacle	65
10 The Universal Administration of Christ in the Heavens	73

PREFACE

This book is composed of messages given by Brother Witness Lee in Stuttgart, Germany from April 4 through 13, 1980.

CHAPTER ONE

CHRIST IN ASCENSION

Scripture Reading: Acts 2:32-33, 36; 5:31; 10:36b; Heb. 4:14-15; 7:25-26; 8:1-2; Rev. 1:5a; Eph. 1:22

I. THE ENDING OF THE BIBLE

The Bible has a wonderful ending! Of course, the beginning is also wonderful. The Bible opens with God and then with His creation. The center of the creation was man, who was made in God's image and after His likeness. If you consider, you will realize that man was formed specifically that he might be one with God. There is also in the opening pages of the Bible the tree of life. When you turn to the end of the Bible, however, you can see that it is even more excellent than the beginning. It may surprise you, but this ending begins with the book of Acts and continues right through the book of Revelation!

When I was young, my mother used to tell us stories from the four Gospels. After I grew up, I found out that when Catholic missionaries went from Italy to China some three or four hundred years ago, the main books they put out were the four Gospels. Even during my youth, missionaries usually preached and taught from these four books. Why were all the other books of the New Testament neglected? It was due to a lack of understanding and appreciation for the ending of the Bible.

Now we are here in Europe at the latter part of the twentieth century. It is time to see how the Bible ends. What is the real ending of God's revelation? To see His revelation in creation is easy. To see His salvation is also not too difficult. But to see the final stage of His revelation is not easy.

There are three main ministries in this final stage. No

doubt there are some minor ones as well, but we shall be concerned with only these three major ones. The first is the ministry of Christ in the heavens. The second is the completing ministry of Paul. Without Paul's Epistles, the Bible clearly is not completed. Yes, much has been revealed already, but it takes Paul's ministry to bring to completion the divine revelation. The third is John's mending ministry. Though the completing writing was done by Paul, damage came in, and there was therefore the need of John's ministry to repair the damage. Paul's last Epistle was written about A.D. 65; it was not until a quarter century later that John's last writing was done.

If we want to know God's up-to-date move, we surely must understand the conclusion of the Bible. It is not just one verse, or one chapter, or even one book. There are more than ten books to this ending. With this message we shall begin a series on the first ministry of this final stage.

II. THE EARTHLY VERSUS THE HEAVENLY MINISTRY

The Lord Jesus surely had a fruitful life during the thirty-three and a half years He was on earth. Most of what He accomplished, however, was in a three-year period. Thirty years He spent in preparation. Then He came forth to minister. What is preached and taught among Christians today largely concerns this earthly ministry.

When I was a young, seeking Christian, I was taught that Christ has finished His work. John 19:30 was cited as proof of this. The Lord's word, spoken when He was on the cross, was "It is finished!" After His death He rested in the tomb for three days. Then He was resurrected and ascended to the heavens, not to work but to sit there. To sit, they explained to me, meant that the work was finished. He is there now, waiting till God puts His enemies under His feet (Acts 2:34-35).

Is this the true picture? Has Christ finished His ministry? We have to say both yes and no. Yes, His earthly ministry is finished. But His heavenly ministry still continues.

The Person of Christ has two aspects, as does His ministry. While He was on earth, He was the man Jesus. Since His ascension into heaven, however, He is the glorified Christ.

His earthly ministry lasted for only a limited time, thirty-three and a half years at most. His heavenly ministry, in contrast, is eternal; it will never end.

It is regrettable that many Christians pay attention only to the first part of Christ's ministry. In these messages we want to focus on the second part, which is far more crucial. God's intention is to have a church and, ultimately, the New Jerusalem. During Christ's earthly ministry the church did not come into being, much less the New Jerusalem. The church and the New Jerusalem are not to be seen in the four Gospels.

It is when we come to Acts that we find the church. In Acts, the first book of the ending of the Bible, the church comes into existence, and in the final book, Revelation, the New Jerusalem appears. Yes, in Acts there is the preaching of the gospel, but that is not an end in itself. The preaching of the gospel is for the producing of the church. The church is the outstanding feature of Acts. Then in the last book of the ending, the first two chapters pertain to the churches, but in the last two chapters there is the New Jerusalem, which is the ultimate consummation of the churches. If we take a bird's-eye view of the books from Acts to Revelation, we shall find that the church and the New Jerusalem stand out the most.

The church and the New Jerusalem are carried out by Christ's heavenly ministry, not His earthly one. His earthly ministry accomplished redemption for the producing of the church, but a higher, richer, wider ministry is needed for the carrying out of God's eternal purpose concerning the church and the New Jerusalem. As far as His earthly ministry is concerned, all has been accomplished. Redemption has been secured by the cross. This accomplishment, however, has only ushered Him into His heavenly ministry. Now He is engaged in a more far-reaching ministry than He ever had on earth.

Do not think that the Lord Jesus is seated in the heavens with nothing to do! He is administrating the affairs of the universe! During His earthly life, this is surely not what He was doing. He suffered, was persecuted, and eventually went to the cross to accomplish redemption. Now, all has changed.

He is fully in charge. He is working for you, for the churches, and even for Germany!

The title Christ means the anointed one. He is referred to as God's Anointed (Psa. 2:2; Acts 4:26). When and how was Christ anointed? It was at His baptism, when the Spirit of God descended upon Him. There in the Jordan River, right after He was baptized, God anointed Him with the heavenly oil, that is, the Spirit. This anointing signified His appointment by God.

When did Christ take office? After the President of the United States is elected (corresponding to Christ's appointment), he is inaugurated into office. Two or three months after the election, there is an inaugural ceremony, when he is inducted into office and officially begins his duties. When did Christ's inauguration take place? It was in the ascension. When Christ was exalted to the third heaven, that exaltation was His inauguration into His official position.

During His incarnation, as recorded in the four Gospels, we can see a little man from Nazareth named Jesus. Today, however, He is gloriously different! Is our Christ the Jesus of the Gospels, or the One in ascension? In Levitical times the offerings which the people brought could be different. Some might bring a bullock, others a lamb, and still others just two small turtledoves. This is a picture to us that in our experience Christ may be large like a bullock or small like a turtledove. He is the same Christ, but our enjoyment of Him differs according to our knowledge, appreciation, and experience of His different aspects. For too long we have known Christ only in His incarnation. Now we must know Him in His ascension.

It is strange that so much emphasis is put upon the birth of Christ. From now on you must look away from the manger and away from the carpenter's home and see Christ on the throne in the heavens! Is your Christ still in the manger? Do you treasure the manger, or do you appreciate the throne? Where is your Christ now? You may reply that He is in you. Of course, I must agree because Paul says, "Christ in you, the hope of glory" (Col. 1:27)! But how do you experience this Christ in you? If your appreciation is of the manger, your experience will be limited by that. If your appreciation of Him is linked to the throne, this will uplift the experience you have of Him in your spirit.

When I visited the Vatican, I saw many scenes with a manger. It might be reasonable to see a manger in Bethlehem, but why should manger scenes be so prominent elsewhere? People are being given the impression that Christ is linked with the manger. They have little realization that today He is on the throne. Their concept of Christ is therefore limited to His incarnation. We need to be brought out of that low concept and see Christ in His ascension.

III. THE OFFICES OF THE ASCENDED CHRIST

When Christ ascended, He was inaugurated into a number of great offices.

A. The Christ

Not until His ascension was Christ officially inaugurated as the Christ. On the day of Pentecost Peter said, "God hath made that same Jesus, whom ye have crucified, both Lord and Christ" (Acts 2:36). That verse used to bother me. Was He not Christ before His ascension? Yes, even in eternity He was Christ, but in eternity He was not anointed. It was at His baptism that He was anointed. However, He was not officially inaugurated as the Christ until His ascension. Christ has been not only chosen, appointed, and anointed by God, but also inaugurated by Him into His office. He has passed through the manger, the River Jordan, and the cross, and is now enthroned in the heavens as the Christ.

Everywhere in Christianity the cross can be seen. There are crosses of wood, gold, stone, or steel. Catholics often make the sign of the cross. They have a dead Christ. Their knowledge of Him is limited to the manger and the cross. Where is the symbol of the throne? Our Christ did not end with the crucifixion. He is enthroned! Even in our spirit, there is this throne. The One in our spirit is not lying in a manger nor hanging on the cross, but seated on the throne. It is this enthroned Christ we must experience.

B. Lord

Acts 2:36 also tells us that He was made Lord. Yes, He was Lord before His ascension, but again He was not inaugurated into this office. One of the Old Testament names for God is Lord (Heb., *Adonai*), meaning master. Christ in the Old Testament was Adonai. Then He became a man, a despised Nazarene. This very One was appointed Lord, even when He was on this earth. But it was not until His ascension that He was inaugurated into His lordship. When Peter said, "He is Lord of all" (Acts 10:36) in the house of Cornelius, he meant that He was Lord of all peoples—both Jews and Gentiles—and of all things. There is not only God but a Man on the throne today, who in His ascension was inaugurated as Lord of all!

C. Ruler

"Him hath God exalted with his right hand to be a Prince and a Saviour" (Acts 5:31). The Greek word translated here as Prince is used only four times in the New Testament and always in reference to Christ (Acts 3:15; 5:31; Heb. 2:10, Captain; 12:2, Author). It has been translated a number of different ways in various versions, because there is no precise English equivalent to the Greek. The thought is that this One is the origin and the Originator, the Author, the Leader, and the Inaugurator. He is therefore above all, and spontaneously is the Ruler with authority.

Acts 3:15 calls Him the Prince of life. Here it seems better to translate Prince as Author, or Originator, of life. In Hebrews 2:10 this same word is translated Captain. Christ in ascension is the Captain of our salvation, leading us into glory where He has already entered as the Pioneer. Hebrews 12:2 calls Him the Author of faith. Again, the thought is included that He is the Originator, the Leader, or the Forerunner, of faith. To be our source of faith and to lead us in the pathway of faith are functions of the office into which He has been inaugurated!

How rich is this Christ in ascension! On earth He was so poor that He had to ask water of a Samaritan woman. Now the poverty of His earthly life is over. He has taken office as the origin and the Originator, the Ruler, the Author, the Leader, the Captain, the Pioneer, and the Forerunner! He is far above all. He is the first. All things and all power are in His hands.

D. Savior

When Christ was on earth, He saved Peter, John, and many others. However, although the title Savior is applied to Christ in His earthly ministry (John 4:42), He was not officially the Savior until His ascension (Acts 5:31). Do you realize that your salvation is more glorious than Peter's? Peter was saved unofficially by the Carpenter from Nazareth. You were saved officially by Christ on the throne. I realize you think Peter was special to have been saved by Jesus by the seashore of Galilee, but you were saved by One in glory, One seated on the throne in the third heaven! Do not be envious of Peter! When he was saved, he followed Jesus in Galilee. When you were saved, you were seated with Him in the heavenlies (Eph. 2:6)! Christ has saved you from the throne and to the throne. This is your Savior!

E. High Priest

We have a great High Priest who has passed through the heavens (Heb. 4:14-15)! He is not just a priest, but a High Priest, "able to save to the uttermost those who come forward to God through Him, seeing He is always living to intercede for them" (Heb. 7:25). Christ appears before God on our behalf, praying for us that we may be saved and brought fully into God's eternal purpose. As verse 26 says, He is not only in heaven but "higher than the heavens."

F. Minister

In Hebrews 8:2 Christ is called "a Minister of the holy places, even of the true tabernacle, which the Lord pitched, not man." He is the enthroned Servant, ministering to us from the heavens.

G. Firstborn of the Dead

This is a great title. Lazarus was resurrected from the

dead (John 11:43-44), but his resurrection was only temporary. Later on he died. With the Lord's resurrection, however, death is over. He will live forever. Thus He is truly the Firstborn of the dead (Rev. 1:5).

H. Ruler of the Kings of the Earth

He is also called in Revelation 1:5 the Ruler of the kings of the earth. "Ruler" here is a slightly different word than the title we referred to in Acts 3:15. It is common to call Jesus the King of kings, but to call Him the Ruler of kings is to say that He is far above the earthly rulers.

I. Head over All Things

When Christ was raised from among the dead, God "subjected all things under His feet, and gave Him to be Head over all things to the church" (Eph. 1:22).

These are some of the offices into which Christ was inaugurated in His ascension.

CHAPTER TWO

CHRIST IN GOD'S ADMINISTRATION

Scripture Reading: Rev. 4:1-5; 5:1-10; Matt. 28:18-19; Mark 16:19-20; Acts 1:8; 2:33

THE ASCENSION SCENE

Revelation 4 and 5 used to be a great puzzle to me. As far as I can recall, I never heard any message on them, and it was quite a long time before I came to have some understanding of what they meant. These two chapters present a scene in the opened heavens. There is a throne where God is sitting, surrounded by twenty-four other thrones. There are twenty-four angels as elders in the universe and four living creatures. No doubt there are also myriads of angels present, as well as all the other created beings. This picture declares that God on the throne is the center of the universe.

Then John saw a scroll in the hand of the One sitting on the throne. When the question was raised as to who could open the scroll, John wept that no one was qualified to do so. "Do not weep," one of the elders told him, "the Lion of the tribe of Judah, the Root of David, has overcome to open the scroll and its seven seals" (Rev. 5:5). When John looked, what he saw was a Lamb with seven eyes. This Lion-Lamb was standing, not sitting, and His seven eyes were flashing. From this picture it is clear that His work is not finished. What was finished in John 19 was the work of redemption. But His standing position and His seven flashing eyes both indicate He is taking action.

"And He came and took" the scroll "out of the right hand of Him Who sits upon the throne" (Rev. 5:7). This is the beginning of Christ's ministry in the heavens. Without these two chapters we would not know what happened when Christ ascended to the heavens. From Revelation 4 and 5 we learn that when Christ ascended, He went directly to the throne at the center of the universe. Before the throne, before the twenty-four elders, and surrounded by all the created beings, He received a commission to carry out God's economy, symbolized by that scroll.

We enjoy singing the hymn which is based on Revelation 5:12-13:

> Blessing and honor and glory be Thine,
> And glory be Thine, And glory be Thine.
> Blessing and honor and glory be Thine,
> Both now and evermore.
> *Hymns,* #241

The blessing, honor, and glory are for the Lamb, not on the cross but standing before the throne at the center of the universe, receiving a universal commission! We must not be so shallow as to confine our praises to Christ for redemption only. Our vision must be uplifted to see this Lamb accomplishing a work of eternally vast dimensions.

Consider this photograph that John has taken for us. The redeeming Lamb is now standing at the center of the universe, before God's throne. This tells us that the Redeemer is now in God's administration. He is the Administrator of the universe, executing God's economy. He is not sitting or sleeping there. He is standing, His seven eyes flashing, watching, searching, and even burning. The whole universe is watching this scene. The four living creatures, the twenty-four elders, myriads of angels, and all other creatures are wide awake, alert, observing. These are the circumstances in which they proclaim, "To Him Who sits upon the throne and to the Lamb, be the blessing and the honor and the glory and the might forever and ever" (Rev. 5:13).

How do we know that this scene took place at the time when Christ ascended? We conclude this from 5:6, where the Lamb is described as "having been slain." The Greek here implies that He had just recently been slain. Right after His sacrificial death, He received the universal and eternal commission from God's hand.

THE TWOFOLD WORK OF CHRIST

In His earthly ministry Christ accomplished redemption. Now in His heavenly ministry He is raising up God's building. Redemption is for God's building. The center of this building is the church. Its ultimate consummation is the New Jerusalem. Today the church is a house (1 Tim. 3:15), but that house will consummate in a city. When this happens, God's building is completed. The work of redemption was finished in John 19. A few chapters later, in Acts 2, the building work began. This is the work that continues today.

These two aspects of the work of Christ are not generally known among Christians today. They are familiar with the work of redemption, but if you tell them that Christ is still working in the heavens to accomplish God's building, they may wonder at the strange doctrines you hold! How marvelous it is to be in the light and to see this heavenly view which is hidden from the eyes of most Christians! There is a Lion-Lamb standing in the center of the universe with seven flashing, burning eyes! He saves you from your silence, your coldness, and your laziness!

THE CORRESPONDENCE BETWEEN HEAVEN AND EARTH

Who can thwart this Lion-Lamb? Who can stop the Lord's recovery? The recovery is not part of traditional Christianity. I do believe that what the Lord is doing in the heavens finds its correspondence among us in His recovery. On the day of Pentecost, the response to Christ's move in the heavens began on earth. Only one hundred twenty people were there at the start, most of them simple people from Galilee, not scholars. That work, which began then, is what we are part of today. The work did not begin in China, but in Jerusalem! We are here in our day reflecting what Christ is doing in the heavens.

Wherever we are, we make trouble for Christianity. This is a country with a long-standing Christian tradition. Now a young man has come to stir up trouble! Since 1971 he has been here in Europe, disturbing and upsetting traditional religion.

I first met him in Manila in 1950, when he was just a small boy. Ten years later we had a mountain retreat in Baguio in the Philippines. He attended that young people's conference. There were over a hundred present, and all were set on fire, including him. Eight years later, after I had come to the United States, I received a letter from him. He was studying medicine in Germany, but was burdened to give up medical school to serve the Lord full time. He asked what I would advise. He had already contacted a famous preacher, whose advice was that he should continue his studies. After much prayer I replied that if he felt led of the Lord, he could come to Los Angeles that summer for a training and conference we would be having there. Afterwards there would be about one hundred thirty saints going on a trip to visit the churches in the Far East, including Manila. He did come to Los Angeles, stayed for the conference, and then joined the trip to the Far East.

When we got to Manila, his parents invited me over for a feast. They begged me to charge him to go back to Germany and finish his medical studies. He could serve the Lord, but first he must finish his studies. My reply was that I had not instigated him to drop his studies; we had been out of touch for eight years. He himself felt he could not continue studying, but must serve the Lord. They still entreated me, declaring that I was the only one who could influence him to change his mind. I did not say yes or no, but I did indicate to them that what they proposed was not my job, not my business, but concerned the Lord's work.

This young man was not moved by his family. He went back to Los Angeles and remained there for three years. Then in 1971 the burden fell upon him to come back to Germany, not for his schooling but for the Lord's recovery. Whatever the opposition, the seven eyes have been like a motor inside him. Nothing can quench him!

AUTHORITY AND RULERSHIP

When Christ was ready to ascend to the heavens, He met

with His disciples on a mountain and said to them, "All authority has been given to Me in heaven and on earth. Go therefore and disciple all the nations, baptizing them into the name of the Father and of the Son and of the Holy Spirit" (Matt. 28:16-19). The Lord's charge to the disciples to preach the gospel was a reflection of the authority He had been given both in heaven and on earth (see also Mark 16:19-20).

With this authority He has charged us to disciple the nations. His first commission to the disciples was to go with His authority. I can testify to you that when I became clear that I should begin the work in the United States, I had the deep conviction that I would be there with Christ's authority. I was just a little man from China, with no prestige nor financial backing, but I arrived in the United States with the conviction that Christ's authority was with me.

For Christ to have His gospel preached to the uttermost parts of the earth requires His leadership. As the Ruler of the kings of the earth, the whole earth is under His dominion. He has ordered world events and everyday human affairs for the spread of the gospel.

AN EXAMPLE OF CHRIST'S RULERSHIP

Let me illustrate this for you subjectively. Over fifty years ago in China a group of young people were raised up by the Lord. We were the young generation, striving to get a modern education in order to rescue and build up our country. The leaders of both the Nationalist and Communist parties were all the same age as we were. We were all attending college at the same time, seriously pursuing the knowledge of science, politics, and economics. I started studying English, for example, right after World War I ended in 1918. Some of that generation were captured by communism; we were captured by Christ.

We came to love the Lord and His Word. We studied the Bible, as well as the classic spiritual writings, church history, and the biographies of the spiritual giants from the second century right down to our day. From our research we came to know what Christianity was, and the Lord opened our eyes to see some light in His Word. The first little meeting, or church, was established in 1922. We did not have an easy time of it, but the Lord brought us through and spread His recovery.

After World War II the recovery became prevailing in China. There were about four to six hundred churches scattered throughout the thirty-three provinces. We had no thought to come to the Western world. A great work lay ahead of us, a nation of seven hundred million people of one language. Our only burden was for this people, but we did realize that what the Lord had shown us would one day be brought to the Western world.

We considered that the Lord's move is like the circulation of the blood in the body. Firstly, the Lord sent some from the Western world to bring the gospel to China. Then, there in that pagan country, the Lord raised us up and opened the Bible to us. We realized that what we saw was far beyond what the missionaries had brought. Some day, we believed, the circulation in the Body which had begun from the West would flow back with something from the East. This, we thought, would be through others, not through us. Our hands were full.

Within a short time, however, in 1948 and 1949 the whole situation in China changed. We were bothered and puzzled at this turn of events. The decision was made that I leave mainland China. Where I should go I did not know, but I went to Taiwan.

That small island, primitive in every way, fully discouraged and disappointed me. I had been working in Shanghai, the largest city in the Far East, with six million people. Taiwan seemed insignificant and backward. One day, however, I traveled by train throughout the island. The Lord burdened me and said, "Do not think this place is too small. I will use this island. You begin to work." Within six years, between 1949 and 1955, our number went from less than five hundred to twenty thousand. During that time I was spending about four months of the year in the Philippines and eight months in Taiwan.

Then in 1958 I was invited to visit England and Denmark. On the way I passed through the United States. Two years later the Lord again brought me to the United States. Then in 1962 He brought me there again and this time kept me there. I was gradually being impressed. After a while, I became clear that instead of returning to the Far East, I should begin the ministry in the United States. At the end of 1962 we began. We had no organization nor financial backing, but we began.

This story shows the Lord's rulership. He arranged international events so that we had to come to the United States, even though this was far from my intention.

My thoughts were otherwise. Before the end of World War II, I realized that Japan would be defeated and that China and the United States would win the war. I picked up a burden to evangelize inner Mongolia and drew up a plan to develop this northwest region. I was living in north China, where we had a good number of saints who could provide the manpower. We had nurses, medical doctors, schoolteachers, and merchants. The financial needs would be supplied by some quite wealthy brothers in the northeast of China, which is Manchuria. My plans were well thought out. The co-workers called me the General Director of the Three Norths Corporation! There was north China, the northeast, and the northwest. China did win the war, but contrary to our expectations, the Communists gained control of the country. My dreams for the Three Norths Corporation vanished, though there were some seventy saints who did migrate to inner Mongolia.

Recently I heard news regarding those seventy! A co-worker, one of the elders in my home town, took the lead in that migration in 1943. Now thirty-seven years later, he is still alive, though he has been imprisoned fifteen times. Now there is some freedom, and there are a number of churches in that district. I was happy to hear the news, even though I never got the opportunity to go there myself.

My intention was to go to the northwest, but the Lord sent me to the southeast! I was headed for inner Mongolia, near Siberia, but the Lord sent me to Taiwan, Manila, the United States, and now to Europe. How could this be? This Jesus in the heavens is the Ruler of all kings. He manages every nation. How He manages is absolutely right. He has sent us to spread His recovery, to gain more people for Himself. Fifteen years ago did you ever imagine the Lord could so move in Germany? In our midst we have Italians, Spaniards, Frenchmen, and British, as well as the Germans. Thirty-one years ago I would have died for the Three Norths! But the Lord restrained me from going there. I did not need to die! Now I am here in Europe, enjoying the voices of so many different nationalities.

Who has arranged all this? The heavenly Christ. It is not your doing, nor is it mine. I am too little to have arranged any of it. We praise the Lord for this reflection of His heavenly ministry!

Within a few years the recovery will saturate the whole of Europe. I believe it will invade all the leading cities. Before too long it will even spread back to Jerusalem. From Stuttgart it will go south to Athens, then across the sea to Jerusalem. This is where the church began, and in this age it will return there! This is the Lord's move from the heavens, reflected on this earth.

CHAPTER THREE

CHRIST IN THE BUILDING UP OF THE CHURCH

Scripture Reading: Acts 2:33; 7:55-56; 9:10-16; Eph. 1:20-22; 4:8, 11-12, 15-16

Of the various offices into which Christ was inaugurated at His ascension, the two greatest are that He is the Ruler of the kings of the earth (Rev. 1:5) and the Head over all things to the church (Eph. 1:22).

CHRIST AS RULER

As Ruler of kings, He is administering all the governments on this earth. The purpose of this administration is no doubt the spreading of the gospel. By this means God's chosen ones are being gathered in. From studying world history we can see that the course of events has been for the spread of the gospel. Our common calendar, which is in worldwide usage, is based on the birth of Christ. Even atheistic countries, like Russia and China, use this calendar, thus implying that they are under Christ's sovereign ruling. According to Christ's calendar, we are in the year 1980. This date does not refer to the Roman Caesars nor to the Russian Czars, but to the number of years since Christ's birth. Our Christ is Ruler over the whole earth for the spread of His gospel!

The Lord's Sovereign Rule over Our Work

I would like to testify of this from my own experience. Toward the end of World War II I told the saints that China would be liberated from Japan, that it would become a republic, and that we would have freedom. This did happen. Japan surrendered unconditionally in 1945. We exulted in our freedom. From 1946 through 1948 the gospel preaching among us quickly spread far and wide. In 1948 a missionary traveled throughout China and then reported to his mission that the gospel work was in the hands of the "little flock" (as they referred to the churches) and that it was so prevailing there was no need to send foreign missionaries. This was truly the case. I was in Shanghai in those days. How happy we were! The churches numbered four to six hundred throughout China. One day in Tsingtao, a former German concession and a beautiful modern seaport, over seven hundred were baptized. In the 1930s the number of those baptized was quite small, rarely more than ten. After 1945, however, the number baptized at one time was usually over one hundred. Our joy was short-lived. Almost overnight, it seemed, the political situation changed, and from 1949 the work was very much frustrated.

I left in April 1949 and from that time had no open correspondence with those I knew there. All these years I grieved over that great work. Watchman Nee was imprisoned in 1950 and died in prison in 1972. I was heartbroken, fearing that the whole work was lost. My only comfort was that, through the loss of the work in China, the Lord brought His recovery to the United States, and then to Europe, South America, Africa, and Australasia. But whenever I thought about the work in China, my heart ached. Many of my contemporary co-workers died in prison after spending years there. Brother Nee's term was the longest. He died the day before he was due to be released.

In 1979 the situation changed once again. The United States and China opened diplomatic relations. Red China opened its doors to visitors. Now the news has come out. My heart is no longer aching; it is leaping for joy! I have learned that in some cities from 1949 the Lord's table was never stopped. The saints on the Mainland consider the years from 1949 to 1970 as a time when the church was dormant. Then in 1970 a new generation, born and educated under the present government, came of age. Some of these young people were raised up by the Lord and became prevailing. Even though they had no Bibles, just some written verses, they began to preach the gospel.

The response was overwhelming. The way had been prepared for the gospel! The new generation of the church began to preach by teaching the young people a gospel song. These empty young people loved singing songs about Jesus! In addition, many sick people were miraculously healed. Thousands of young people believed. The officials made things difficult for them, but it had no effect. They imprisoned some of the believers, but there were too many, mostly in the countryside. If ten were imprisoned, two hundred would go to visit. Prison, they told the officials, was to be preferred, because then they did not have to work! They could simply sing the hymns. If they were released, they would believe all the more! In one province there were over three hundred thousand believers. In just one city there were over twenty thousand.

I say this to show you that the Lord Jesus is the Ruler of kings. I thought China with its nine hundred million people was lost, as far as the gospel was concerned. Last year, however, the world situation and China's need caused her to open up. Is this not the Lord's government? Praise Him!

His office as Ruler is primarily for the spread of the gospel. By the Lord's control of the world situation, the recovery has come to the Western world. Now, after thirty years, His sovereign hand has caused the doors of China to open again. Hundreds of thousands of young people have been saved. Who can hinder the Ruler of kings? This is 1980, the year of the Lord, according to His calendar! The Red Chinese government last year printed a hundred thousand copies of the Bible. They have also opened the doors of the cathedrals in the leading cities for the Christians to meet there. In Shanghai over fifteen hundred crowded into the first building they opened. They have since opened two more. All these events prove that Jesus is the Ruler of kings! He is carrying out His heavenly ministry. He is administrating the whole earth that the gospel may be spread.

CHRIST AS HEAD

In addition to His sovereignty over the nations, Christ also exercises His headship. As Head over all things to the church, He works to gain His chosen vessels.

Gaining Saul

Let us consider just one vessel, Saul of Tarsus. If we read Acts 9, we can see how much Christ did to win Saul. He Himself came purposely to gain him. He had even more to say to him through Ananias (vv. 10-17). Though His intention in Acts 9 was to capture Saul, His words to Ananias were more detailed. Notice how busy the Lord was, just to gain one vessel. He appeared to Saul as he traveled to Damascus. Then He gave Saul a vision that Ananias would come and restore his sight. Then He went to Ananias in a vision and conversed with him about going to see Saul, who, He said, "is a chosen vessel unto me, to bear my name before the Gentiles, and kings, and the children of Israel: For I will show him how great things he must suffer for my name's sake" (Acts 9:15-16).

Why did the Lord spend so much effort for just one person? The purpose of Saul's being gained was the building up of the Body of Christ. There was the need of such a vessel. Yes, there was Peter, and James, and John. But they were not sufficient. The Lord still had need of one like Saul. Thus He Himself stepped in to win this one vessel.

Gaining Us

Do not take your being saved as a small thing. It was accomplished because the Lord Jesus exercised His rulership. He arranged that you should be born in the country in which you were born. Your place of birth was not accidental, but under His administration. You were born in the right country, the right town, the right family, and at the right time He brought you to Himself. You may have been in Switzerland, or Germany, or France, or Spain, or Denmark, or Norway, or England. One day He arranged for you to be at a certain spot, and you repented, believed, and were saved. If you had been in Moscow, the opportunity to be saved and now to be meeting here, might not have come to you. It was under the King's rulership that you got saved!

Do you think that the Lord has finished His work with you? No! By His rulership you were saved. Now His headship comes in. Consider how it is that you are attending these meetings here. You have come from all over Europe; some have even followed me from the United States. What has brought you? There is no entertainment, no beautiful music; only two-and-a-half-hour meetings with a Chinese speaking! To an outsider what is attracting you is incomprehensible. Yet some of you would have wept if you had not been able to come! How do you account for this? It is that you are now under Christ's headship, which is not only over you like His rulership, but within you. He is the Head over all things to the church (Eph. 1:22). Your coming together here is the Lord's doing.

Building Up His Body

The dear Lord is working. He is not merely sitting in the heavens. When Stephen was stoned to death, Jesus was standing at the right hand of God (Acts 7:55-56), watching over and caring for His members. To persecute a believer was to persecute Him. He said to Saul, "Saul, Saul, why persecutest thou me?...I am Jesus whom thou persecutest" (Acts 9:4-5). Stephen was part of Him. So was Peter. Every member, every believer in Him, is part of Him. He is caring for them all. He is working in each one, that they might all be useful. He is making them apostles, prophets, evangelists, and shepherds and teachers, that they might be equipped to perfect the saints, so that the Body might be built up.

Here in Europe is a good example of how the Lord is working to build up His Body. Less than ten years ago, one brother came without backing from any mission board. The Lord's recovery came to Europe with no organization. Yet the Lord has moved, and the recovery has spread to many European countries. Still today there is no organization, yet the work goes forward. One young man came, with no theological degree and not much experience. He came with only the ascended Christ! This heavenly Christ was caring for this little member of His Body ever since 1960, when he attended a young people's conference in the Philippines. When he came to Germany in 1971, it was under this heavenly ministry.

Sending Forth the Perfected Ones

You are all under this dear Christ's heavenly ministry. The day will come when you will be sent out, not by any man, but by the ascended Head! Some of you will go to Austria, some to Greece, and some to Israel with the heavenly ministry of the ascended Christ! Christ's working is not slow. The recovery has been in the Western world only seventeen years. Yet it has spread to North, Central, and South America; to Africa; to Europe; and to Australasia. In the Far East there are churches in Japan, Korea, Taiwan, the Philippines, Singapore, Malaysia, Thailand, and Indonesia. Hundreds of churches have been raised up without any organization. Whose doing is this? It is the work of the ascended Christ!

We in ourselves cannot build the church. Under His heavenly ministry, however, we can be equipped to be useful members in His Body. The Body itself is built up directly from the supply of the Head. "Wherefore He says, having ascended to the height, He led captive those taken captive and gave gifts to men...And He gave some apostles, and some prophets, and some evangelists, and some shepherds and teachers, for the perfecting of the saints unto the work of ministry, unto the building up of the Body of Christ" (Eph. 4:8, 11-12). When Christ ascended to the heavens, He gave gifts—apostles, prophets, evangelists, and teachers and shepherds. These gifts perfect the saints, so that in every local church the members are edified, equipped, and qualified to function.

As every part of the Body functions, we "grow up into Him in all things, Who is the Head, Christ, out from Whom all the Body, fitted and knit together through every joint of the supply, according to the operation in measure of each one part, causes the growth of the Body unto the building up of itself in love" (Eph. 4:15-16). All the members grow into the Head. Then out from the Head the supply will come that the Body may be built up. This is the way the local churches are built up by the supply of the Head.

The Head is busy ministering. While we are meeting here, receiving what is ministered out of Him, He is ministering there, taking care of all the members of the churches. The

Lord's recovery is not just another Christian work. It is a reflection of His ministry in the heavens! It corresponds to what the ascended Christ is doing there. We are cooperating and coordinating with the heavenly ministry of the ascended Christ!

A SUMMARY

His ministry, as we have seen, is twofold. On the one hand, He is administering the whole world as Ruler of the kings of the earth in order that His gospel may be spread and God's chosen people be gathered together. On the other hand, as the Head of the Body, He is ministering to edify, equip, and qualify His members, so that they in turn may perfect others. Then He will send out some to new places to spread the recovery. Hallelujah for this heavenly ministry!

CHAPTER FOUR

CHRIST IN THE GROWTH AND FUNCTION OF THE BELIEVERS FOR THE BUILDING UP OF THE BODY

Scripture Reading: Eph. 4:7-16; Col. 2:19

We have been considering the Lord as Ruler and Head. As Ruler He has been controlling the whole earth. He has been directing the affairs of all the nations for the spreading of the gospel and the gathering in of God's people. This rulership implies His moving on this earth. He is carrying out a great move. When we consider Him as Head, in addition to His moving we realize that the matter of life is brought in. Under Christ's headship, a very fine work in life is being done. We do not know the details of Christ's heavenly ministry as Ruler moving on earth. When we come to His ministry as Head, however, we see a fine work in life, by life, and with life.

TWO ASPECTS OF CHRIST'S HEADSHIP

In Ephesians 4 we can see two categories in this fine work of life. The first is Christ's giving of gifts for the perfecting of the saints (vv. 8-12). "He gave some apostles, and some prophets, and some evangelists, and some shepherds and teachers, for the perfecting of the saints." The second category is His making all the saints grow that they may function. By this growth and functioning, the Body is directly built up. "But holding to truth in love, we may grow up into Him in all things, Who is the Head, Christ, out from Whom all the Body, fitted and knit together through every joint of the supply, according to the operation in measure of each one part, causes the growth of the Body unto the building up of itself in love" (vv. 15-16).

For both these categories the headship is working. It is the headship of Christ which produces the gifts that the members may grow and function. This is a fine work in life.

Christianity's way of operating is absolutely contrary to this. They establish seminaries; hire professors to teach the Bible, theology, church history, Hebrew and Greek; then hope the students will be perfected as preachers, ministers, pastors, and such. Their trust is in an educational system. History has already demonstrated that the Body of Christ cannot be built up in this way, Paul was not a seminary graduate. It was under the headship of Christ alone that he was raised up to be the most useful apostle.

THE FINE WORK TO GAIN PAUL

How did the headship of Christ operate to gain Paul as a gift to the Body? You will recall that Stephen suffered martyrdom right before the eyes of a young man named Saul of Tarsus (Acts 7:58). Stephen's death was not an isolated, individual matter. At that time the whole Body of Christ was under persecution. Saul was one of the ringleaders; he "made havoc of the church" (Acts 8:1-3). The Head of the Body allowed that persecution to show Saul what the Body of Christ is. Saul saw the Body suffering when he persecuted the members who called on the name of the Lord. After this, he happily began his journey to Damascus intending to arrest still other members. This is the set of circumstances the Head arranged for this apostle-to-be!

Suddenly Jesus stepped in, not from the earth but from the heavens. This Jesus was now "Head over all things to the church, which is His Body"! Saul was shocked to hear the voice saying, "Saul, Saul, why persecutest thou me?" (Acts 9:4). Yes, he was shocked to be confronted by Jesus, but even the more he was shocked to be made aware that the believers he had been persecuting were members of the Body of Christ. Even at his conversion, under the headship of Christ Saul realized the Body.

The Head One with His Body

Saul, of course, did not argue. He did not say, "Lord, I was not persecuting You. I was not persecuting anyone in the heavens. The ones I was trying to get are on earth." Why did Saul not argue? I believe that while the Lord was saying, "I am Jesus whom thou persecutest" (v. 5), the Spirit of the Body was moving in Saul.

Peter's conversion was much simpler than Paul's. Peter was with his brother fishing when the Lord called, "Follow Me, and I will make you fishers of men" (Matt. 4:18-20). That Galilean fisherman had no hesitation in following Him. He liked the thought of becoming a fisher of men, rather than simply catching fish!

Paul's case was far more profound. The way the Lord approached him, asking him that short question, surely set him thinking. Though the words the Lord said to Saul were few, they must have occupied his thoughts during those days immediately after when he could not see. Surely he did not spend those three days sleeping! He must have been greatly troubled by that momentous encounter. Why, he must have wondered, did that voice say, "Why persecutest thou me?" What does *Me* mean? The Spirit of the Body would have told him, *"Me* means the enlarged Christ, the increased Christ, the corporate Christ, the Christ including Peter, James, and Stephen." When Saul asked, "Who are You, Lord?" the reply was, "I am Jesus." But how could that be Jesus? Was Jesus not dead and buried? How could He come now from the heavens?

Showing His Will through the Body

Saul must also have thought on the Lord's words, "Arise, and go into the city, and it shall be told thee what thou must do" (Acts 9:6). Why did the Lord give him such an indirect answer to his question, "What wilt thou have me to do?" Again, the Head was showing him the principle of the Body. Saul was not to know the Lord's will by himself. He would be in the Body and needed to be trained to know the Body. He would learn to trust in his brothers, the other members. The Head had been persecuted by Saul through the Body. Now he would learn to respect the Body. Rather than tell him what to do directly, the Lord would send Ananias, a small disciple, to restore Saul's sight and make His will known to him. It would not be a leading one, like Peter, who would come, but an unknown one. Thus the Lord would subdue Saul and make him a useful apostle.

To again contrast his case with Peter's, notice the simple way in which Peter was made an apostle. Firstly the Lord saw and called him to be a fisher of men. Then, perhaps a year or two later, the Lord simply sent him out with the other eleven, and from that point on he and they were apostles (Matt. 10:1-5). How foolish of the Catholic Church to elevate this simple apostle!

While Saul was in Damascus praying, he saw a vision that Ananias would come and heal his sight. We know nothing of this little disciple prior to this occasion, but the Head knew him and told Saul he would come. Then the Head summoned Ananias. "Arise, and go into the street which is called Straight, and inquire in the house of Judas for one called Saul, of Tarsus: for, behold, he prayeth, and hath seen in a vision a man named Ananias coming in, and putting his hand on him, that he might receive his sight" (Acts 9:10-12). Do you realize how busy Christ was, going back and forth between Saul and Ananias? He was carrying out His heavenly ministry.

Saul Received into the Body

Ananias then went to the house where Saul was staying, laid hands on him, and said, "Brother Saul, the Lord, even Jesus, that appeared unto thee in the way as thou camest, hath sent me, that thou mightest receive thy sight, and be filled with the Holy Spirit" (v. 17). Then Saul received sight, arose, and was baptized. He was baptized not only into Christ, but also into the Body. Then he stayed for some days with the disciples who were in Damascus. Thus he was received into the Body as a brother.

Protected and Cared For by the Body

Saul straightway preached Christ in the synagogues, thus arousing the opposition of the Jews, who finally plotted to kill him (vv. 20-25). How did he escape from Damascus? It was not by putting on a disguise and slipping away. Rather, the members of the Body let him down over the wall by night in a basket. The basket may point to the church. He was sent off in the Body and by the Body.

When Saul came to Jerusalem, the apostles there did not receive him. They suspected he was trying to deceive them and were afraid. Another member, Barnabas, came into the picture, recounting to the apostles how Saul had been genuinely converted. Again, it was through a member of the Body, but not the apostles, that Saul was brought in.

Later Saul went back to Tarsus, his birthplace. It was here that Barnabas found him. Barnabas brought him to Antioch, where they stayed for a year, meeting with the church and teaching the people (Acts 11:25-26).

By all these steps this young opposer eventually became an apostle. This illustrates to us how much time the Lord Jesus spent to make just one believer a useful apostle.

Ephesians 4:8 tells us, "Wherefore He says, Having ascended to the height, He led captive those taken captive and gave gifts to men." To say He gave gifts to men is a simple statement, but we can see from Paul's case how complicated it was for this one member to be made a gift as an apostle. In His ascension Christ exercised His headship to direct His Body, having one member do one part and another member fulfill another part.

Paul's case shows the fine work in life that the ascended Head does to prepare even one useful apostle. Such an operation is not of Christ's move as Ruler; this is a work under His headship, bringing His whole Body into a fine functioning. Do you think Paul could have become an apostle by attending a seminary for four years? It took many members of the Body for the Head to prepare Paul to be an apostle.

Before too long it could well be that a number of you will be sent out as apostles. You must realize that, for this to take place, the Head in the heavens must exercise His headship toward many members in His Body.

THE WAY THE MEMBERS GROW AND FUNCTION

How can all the members grow and function that the Body of Christ might be built up? Suppose a Pentecostal revivalist comes among you. After he preaches some soul-stirring sermons, you are all aroused. You begin to speak in tongues, to roll on the floor, to shout that you have the power, and to preach from the rooftop that the people below must repent and believe in Jesus lest they go to hell. Do you believe that a movement like this can make you grow? I have seen how those in Pentecostalism behave. From my observation I must say that there is little if any growth among them. Pentecostalism is a movement, not the fine work in life that the Head exercises to touch His members one by one in detail after detail.

Please do not misunderstand me. It is not my intention to discredit any Christian work, but I believe the Lord has shown me that Pentecostalism is not the work that can build up His Body in life. It does not accomplish His fine work in life. I have received a burden from the Lord; I do know what He is after. I have the assurance that after just a few days of meeting together, all of you have been touched by the Lord in a fine way. You have gone to the Lord and praised Him for bringing you out of darkness, for touching your heart, and for enlightening you. To thus touch the Lord and be touched by Him is the fine way in life by which you grow.

The result of this growth will be the expression of your function. Function comes from growth, and growth from the fine work in life of the Head.

Notice what Ephesians 4:15-16 says: "But holding to truth in love, we may grow up into Him in all things, Who is the Head, Christ, out from Whom all the Body, fitted and knit together through every joint of the supply, according to the operation in measure of each one part, causes the growth of the Body unto the building up of itself in love." We must all grow into the Head. Then, out of the Head into whom we have grown, we shall have a supply. Whatever part of the Body we are, we shall receive a supply from the Head in order that we may function to minister life to the Body. In this way the Body will be built up.

Colossians 2:19, like the passage in Ephesians, also speaks of "holding the Head, out from Whom all the Body, by means of the joints and bands being supplied and knit together, grows with the growth of God." We may be a joint, for the supply of the Body, or a band, for the knitting together of the members.

The Body has only one Head. Consider how busy He must be to take care of each one of you. His heavenly ministry is to care for you in such a detailed way. He exercises His headship to burden me to come here to minister Him to you. He burdens the elders to get in touch with you. He stirs up some other members who are close to you to fellowship and pray with you. He constrains you to contact Him that He may deal with you and supply you with the particular riches you need. While you are being helped and are enjoying Him, you will grow. Then He may exercise His headship to have you go to Neuchatel. While you are there, you may give a testimony which helps those who are there. All this activity is part of Christ's heavenly ministry, causing all His members to grow and function that His Body may be built up.

AN ORGANIC ENTITY

You will realize that what I am describing to you is an organic relationship between Christ and His Body. You are living members of this organism, not mere members in an organization. This organism has Christ as its Head, exercising His care over each one of you and over all of you mutually. You are all being cared for together under His headship. Praise the Lord that here in Europe there is this organism under Christ's living headship! I trust you can see how different this is from the traditional Christian work. In your physical body, there is no dead arrangement as to how the various parts will function. Every nerve, every muscle, and every member are under the living control of the head. The whole body is under an organic headship.

The activity of the physical body under the direction of the head corresponds to the heavenly ministry of Christ as Head. He does not need a Christian organization to be established for His Body to be built up. He works organically, first to make apostles and then to make all the members grow and function. This work results in the Body building itself up.

My burden under Christ's organic headship is to minister life into you, not to stir you up. I do believe Christ has been ministered into you. If so, you are continually constrained to contact Him. "Lord Jesus, I love You. You are my life. You are all I need. I am open to You. I want to be gained and occupied by You. I would have my whole being saturated with Your very Person." You have probably already been praying like this. If you have, you are under the exercise of Christ's headship, His heavenly ministry, receiving the life He ministers into you for the growth and functioning of His Body.

CHAPTER FIVE

OUR CORRESPONDING TO CHRIST'S HEAVENLY MINISTRY UNDER HIS HEADSHIP

Scripture Reading: Acts 8:26-39; 9:10-11; 10:1-3, 9-22; Col. 2:18-19; Eph. 4:14-16

Ever since His ascension the Lord has been ministering in the heavens. For this ministry to be worked out on the earth, however, requires a correspondence to it on our side. Nearly twenty centuries have gone by, but not much has been fulfilled on earth. Thus, as this age draws to a close, there is an urgent need for us to correspond to the Lord's ministry.

A TWOFOLD CORRESPONDENCE

The verses above illustrate this correspondence on our side. The references in Acts all relate to a move in life for the spread of the gospel. During the time of the Acts, the disciples were moving on with the Lord in life. This was so in the case of Philip and the Ethiopian eunuch; Ananias and Saul; and Peter and Cornelius. All three were moves in life that corresponded to the Lord's ministry in the heavens.

The references in the Epistles, in contrast, illustrate the growth and function in life, rather than a move in life. What is revealed in Ephesians and Colossians is not a move for the gospel, but the growth and function of the Body. The one is to bring people to the Lord; the other, to build up the Body. For people to be brought to the Lord requires a move in life; for the Body to be built up, the growth and function in life is needed.

The move in life to bring people to the Lord is outward, but the growth in life for the building of the Body is inward. For both the outward and the inward aspects, we need to correspond to the Lord's ministry in the heavens.

CORRESPONDING TO THE MOVE IN LIFE

In Acts 8, 9, and 10 the Lord moved His disciples outwardly for the preaching of the gospel. He was ministering in the heavens to move some of His disciples. Suppose Philip at that time had been away loving the world, Ananias had fallen into sin, and Peter had gone back to Galilee to go fishing. Christ would then have been ministering in the heavens, but there would have been no response on earth. Praise the Lord, these three were ready to respond!

Philip

In response to the Lord's heavenly ministry, Philip left Jerusalem for Gaza (Acts 8:26). While he was walking along in the desert, he was responding to the heavenly Christ. The Lord had one disciple there in the desert that He could move. When He said to Philip, "Go near, and join thyself to this chariot" (v. 29), Philip ran there and heard the eunuch reading Isaiah. Do you see how Philip was corresponding to the heavenly ministry? It was through this that the Ethiopian eunuch was brought to the Lord. This was the corresponding on Philip's side to the move in life for the preaching of the gospel.

Ananias

The situation in Acts 9 was similar. Ananias must have been praying, when a vision came to him from the heavens. The Lord spoke to him via heavenly television and directed him to Saul! Saul was also praying, when the heavenly television transmission came to him, and he saw Ananias coming! There was a marvelous triangle of Christ ministering in the heavens, with Ananias and Saul corresponding to it on earth, all aimed at bringing Saul to the Lord.

Peter

In Acts 10 a Roman centurion named Cornelius was praying, when an angel came and told him to send for Peter.

Suppose Peter had been unavailable when the messengers came to him from Cornelius. If Peter had gone fishing, the messengers would have had to return empty-handed and disappointed! As it was, Peter, just before the men arrived, was also praying when the heavenly television transmission came to him! A vessel like a sheet descended from heaven, full of unclean animals. Peter was told, "Rise, kill and eat!" His reply was, "Not so, Lord!" This wonderful television program was repeated three times! While Peter was puzzling over what it meant, the messengers appeared at the gate, asking for him. He went with them, and Cornelius, his family, and probably the soldiers as well, were all brought to the Lord.

This is the proper gospel preaching. It is a move in life under the heavenly ministry of Christ. It is not a movement organized by a mission board. Christ as the Head exercised His headship to move His disciples here and there. They were on the alert, responding to His ministry from the heavens. I hope the preaching of the gospel in the recovery will be like this: a prevailing move in life, corresponding to the Lord's heavenly ministry under His headship.

A Testimony

Let me give you an illustration from my experience regarding this matter.

In July 1932 I had just come back home from my work at the office when a brother came. Actually, he was looking for someone else, but that other brother was away. Since it was still early in the evening, I suggested that the two of us go to the beach. While we were on the way, he raised up some spiritual questions. I said it would be good to sit on the beach and talk over these matters. This we did, conversing from about seven to eleven. We talked about baptism by immersion. (Our denomination practiced sprinkling.)

As soon as we finished our conversation, he said to me, "You are the right person to baptize me. I am the right person to be baptized. You must baptize me tonight!"

I was just a young man, about twenty-seven. I was not a pastor, nor an elder, nor even a deacon. I shrank back. "No, no, no!" I said. "I cannot. I am too young. I am not a pastor, or elder, or deacon. No!"

He rebuked me. "You just preach, but you won't practice. You have been telling me who is the right person to baptize, where is the right place, and what is the right time. I have been considering: here is the right place (the sea is in front of us, full of water), this is the right time (a summer evening), I am the right person to be baptized, and you are the right person to do the baptizing. How can you refuse?"

I was subdued. Even though we had not brought any change of clothing, we went into the water, and I baptized him. After that, we were both in the third heaven!

Two days later, on a Thursday, I was in the office and needed to record his name. I could not remember how it was spelled. Since one of my colleagues knew him quite well, I asked him how the name was spelled. He was curious that I should need to know the spelling, and asked me what had happened.

"You want to know what happened?" I replied. "The night before last I baptized him in the sea!"

He was astonished, but I was astonished also when he said, "You baptized him! Well, I would like you to baptize me too tonight!"

Because there was another colleague who had also been brought to the Lord, I replied, "Let me talk to So-and-so first." When I talked to him, he was happy to join us. After office hours, the three of us went to the beach, along with the brother whom I had baptized earlier. This one I asked to do the baptizing, but he refused. It bothered me: why was I baptizing people, as though I were a pastor? Nonetheless, I baptized the two new ones.

Afterwards, we were rejoicing to the uttermost! We wandered along the streets, talking about the Lord's grace. We made so much noise that a man behind us pursued after us and then asked, "Are you Witness Lee?"

"Yes," I replied. "Why?"

He told us he had just come from a prayer meeting of a mission church, where they were complaining that I had baptized one of their candidates; they said I was neither an elder nor a deacon; how then could I baptize people? Then he added, "When I heard them talking, I decided I would like to get in touch with you. I never dreamed I would find you like this. When will you have the next meeting?"

By the Lord's Day, there were eleven of us. After one week, we began to have the Lord's table. The Lord exercised His headship to bring people in. Though our number was small, we were corresponding to the heavenly Christ. Since those days, much has been accomplished, not by organization, but by His ministering in the heavens and some of His disciples corresponding on earth.

CORRESPONDING FOR THE BUILDING UP OF THE BODY

Now that we have covered some of the wonderful things that transpired in the book of Acts, illustrating the Lord's move in life to gain people through the preaching of the gospel, let us go on to see how the Body is built up. It is the Epistles which deal with this matter. Rather than being accomplished by a move, the building up of the Body comes about through the growth in life. For this finer, deeper work, there needs to be a finer corresponding.

Holding the Head

Christ is the Head, and we are the members. Colossians 2:19 reminds us that we must hold the Head, "out from Whom all the Body, by means of the joints and bands being supplied and knit together, grows with the growth of God." To hold the Head means that there is direct communication between us and Him. There is no separation between Him and all the members. The members correspond to whatever the Head ministers. The result of this correspondence is the growth in life. By holding the Head, there is an inward growth, not an outward move. In this close communication between the Head and the members, all His riches are ministered into the members and all the negative things are swallowed up by the supply of life from the Head.

The way we grow is by holding the Head. Growth does not come about from the study of the Bible or the understanding of doctrine. Such knowledge is not much help to our growth.

The Head is the source of life. When we hold Him, that is, keep ourselves intimately connected to Him, His riches and life supply enter into our being and become our growth in life.

Growing Up into the Head

"But holding to truth in love, we may grow up into Him in all things, Who is the Head, Christ, out from Whom all the Body, fitted and knit together through every joint of the supply, according to the operation in measure of each one part, causes the growth of the Body unto the building up of itself in love" (Eph. 4:15-16). These verses go a step further than Colossians 2:19. We are not only to hold the Head, but also to grow up into Him in all things. To hold the Head is close and intimate, but to grow into Him is a deeper and finer correspondence. Words are inadequate to convey what is meant by this growing up into Him, but perhaps some examples may help us to grasp the thought.

In Marriage

Married life was ordained by God and is to "be held in honor among all" (Heb. 13:4). The sisters surely are pleased to have a husband, and the brothers a wife! If you are not yet married, you no doubt are thinking how wonderful it would be. Marriage is surely a wonderful arrangement! Nonetheless, as one who has been married for over fifty years, I must say that married life is not easy. If you are not married, you are not aware of all the troubles that arise. What is the cause of the problems? Mostly it is because your marriage is still not in the Head. You may be willing to grow into the Lord in everything else, but in the matter of your marriage you would retain yourself. Deep within, you may have the intention to keep your marriage outside the Lord. Some sisters suffer much in their married life because of this. You have a reservation, perhaps never expressed in words, about growing into the Lord in your marriage. Thus, in this point you are not corresponding to Him while He is ministering in the heavens.

In Shopping and in Other Weaknesses

Sisters especially seem to like shopping. Thus they often

have a problem corresponding to the Lord in this matter. The first thing in the morning they may have a wonderful time praying and enjoying the Lord. But right after breakfast they may pick up a newspaper and find some special bargains advertised. The Lord is forgotten! They must go to the stores right away, or the things they want will be sold out! The One who is in the heavens is also within, however. His word is, "Don't go!"

They reply, "Lord, just this one time give me a little liberty!"

Is not this the way you are? In your prayer earlier you were corresponding to Him, but now your desire to go shopping has annulled that corresponding. Now the Lord has no way. He has to suffer, and you will suffer too. If you go shopping this way, you will find it hard to pray afterwards. Two or three days may go by without your being able to pray. For this period of time there is no correspondence on your part to the Lord's heavenly ministry. He is gone, and there is no communication between you and Him during those days.

It is not only the sisters who have such a weakness. I have my weaknesses too. In many things I have grown into the Lord, but in certain other things I also would say, "Lord, all this time I have been loving You. Can I not have just a little rest from loving You? How about giving me a few hours off?" From my own experience I know this is also what happens to you. You do not need to come to talk to me about your weakness. I was once a young man too and had the same kind of weakness. While I was indulging that weakness, I was absent from the Lord, and there was no growth in life.

In Things Great and Small

Sometimes it is in the big things that we find it hard to grow into the Lord; many times, however, it is in the small things. We may think the Lord is not interested in the small things, like how we wear our hair. Whether the matter is big or small, if we do not grow into Him in that thing, our corresponding to Him is arrested. I would say that especially in the small things we must grow into Him. This growth into Him keeps us in direct correspondence to His heavenly ministry under His headship. This ministry requires a very fine correspondence on our part. Then we shall grow.

The Supply from the Head

When we hold the Head and grow up into Him in all things, out from Him will come the life supply to the Body. As we hold Him and grow up into Him, the riches of the Head will flow out through us. I like these two phrases, "into Him" and "out from Him" (see Eph. 4:15-16). There is first the growing into Him; then the life supply will come out of Him. When this is true of us, we are corresponding to the Lord's ministry in the heavens. Then the functions will emerge for the building up of the Body.

GIVING THE LORD A WAY

There is the need for our twofold correspondence to the Lord's heavenly ministry. Among Christians today, at most there seems to be only the move in life for the preaching of the gospel. There is little growth in life for the building up of the Body. We must not neglect either aspect. The Lord needs us to correspond to Him so that He can move in us to bring people to Himself. He also wants our response that we may grow up into Him so that something of Him may come forth to supply and build up the Body.

As we correspond to the Lord's ministry in these two aspects, His will will be fulfilled. If we are short in this corresponding, the Lord has no way to carry out His heavenly ministry. It is crucial for us in the recovery to see this. For the spread of the gospel and for the building up of His Body by the growth in life, the Lord must have our correspondence on earth to what He is ministering in the heavens. We need to pray much for this correspondence.

CHAPTER SIX

HOW WE HOLD THE HEAD
AND GROW INTO HIM IN ALL THINGS

Scripture Reading: Col. 2:18-19; Eph. 4:14-16; Rom. 6:3; 1 Cor. 1:9, 24, 30; 2:2; 15:22, 45; 2 Cor. 3:17-18; Gal. 5:4; Eph. 3:16-17; Phil. 1:21a; 3:8; Col. 1:18; 3:4, 11

The goal of Christ's heavenly ministry is to fulfill God's eternal purpose. What God wants is the church. For the church to be realized, two kinds of work are needed. The first is the move in life in an outward way to preach the gospel and bring people to God. The second is the inward growth in life for the building up of the Body.

In the past centuries this first aspect of the work has been largely accomplished. Many zealous Christians have gone forth as missionaries to spread the gospel. Even up till the present, many seeking Christians are still on this line.

When we come to the building up of the Body, however, we find that this aspect has been neglected. Many Christians do not even know what the growth in life is. Very few know that there is the need for the building up of the Body. Millions of people have been brought to the Lord, but because they have so little growth in life, there is very little building. Few Christians have a concern about this fine, inner work. It is my burden that, regarding this aspect of the Lord's move in the heavens, there may be a finer, deeper correspondence to Him on our part.

Such a correspondence depends upon your holding the Head and growing into Him (Col. 2:19; Eph. 4:15). How much you hold the Head and grow into Him is the factor which determines how much you correspond to Him in the inner life for the building up of the Body. Yet these two crucial terms are probably new to you. Has anyone else ever called your attention to them? Have you ever heard a sermon on how to hold the Head, or one on how to grow into the Head? Christ is your Head. He is the Head of the Body. All the members of the Body must hold the Head and grow into Him in all things.

PAUL'S WRITINGS

Paul's Epistles are in two groups. The sequence in which they are arranged in the Bible is quite meaningful. The first seven Epistles, from Romans to Colossians, form one group. His first Epistles are Romans and 1 and 2 Corinthians. These three are followed by the four which I have called the heart of the divine revelation—Galatians, Ephesians, Philippians, and Colossians. This first group, then, consists of three plus four.

The second group consists of 1 and 2 Thessalonians, 1 and 2 Timothy, Titus, and Philemon. These are six. Of course, there is also the Epistle to the Hebrews, whose authorship has caused much argument. I do believe there is ample evidence to say that Paul was the author. These seven Epistles are of four plus three. The two Thessalonians and the two Timothys make up the four, while Titus, Philemon, and Hebrews are the three. This second group of seven will not concern us in this message.

The first set of seven Epistles deals with three main points: Christ living in us, the all-inclusive Christ, and the church. These are the crucial points in Paul's ministry to complete the Word of God (Col. 1:25). For the completing work to be accomplished, we must experience Christ living in us, we must understand how all-inclusive He is, and we must have the vision of the glorious church. These are the emphases of Paul's first seven Epistles.

Let us see how Paul's writings stress these three points.

A LOOK AT THE FIRST SEVEN EPISTLES

Romans mentions many different matters in its sixteen chapters. According to Martin Luther, however, its main subject is justification by faith. In actuality, it is more accurate to say that its message is that God has transferred us out of

Adam and into Christ. This includes justification by faith. Through our parents we were born in Adam, but when we believed in the Lord Jesus, we were transferred out of the first man and into Christ. Romans 6:3 tells us that we have been baptized into Christ Jesus. Now we are in Him. We are no longer in Adam, but in Christ.

First Corinthians tells us that we have been "called unto the fellowship of his Son Jesus Christ our Lord" (1:9). Many Christians have the low concept that God has called them so that some day they might go to heaven. This verse, however, says that we have been called into the fellowship, or participation, or enjoyment, of Christ. He must be our enjoyment. He is the power and wisdom of God (1:24). Because we are in Him, He is to us "wisdom, and righteousness, and sanctification, and redemption" (1:30). With such a vast Christ to be enjoyed, Paul "determined not to know anything among you, save Jesus Christ, and him crucified" (2:2). In 15:22 Paul further says that "in Christ shall all be made alive." Christ makes us alive because as the last Adam He became a life-giving Spirit (15:45). All these aspects of Christ, presented in this Epistle, are for our enjoyment and are accessible to us because He has become the life-giving Spirit.

Second Corinthians continues this thread that the Lord is now the Spirit (3:17). Our part is to take away the veils that we may behold and reflect Him. "But we all, with unveiled face beholding and reflecting as a mirror the glory of the Lord, are being transformed into the same image from glory to glory, even as from the Lord Spirit" (3:18, lit.). As we look unto Him and reflect Him, we are being transformed into His image from glory to glory, even as from the Lord Spirit. This term, the Lord Spirit, is a compound title referring to Christ.

Paul warned the Galatian believers that if they tried to keep the law, they would be brought to nought from Christ (Gal. 5:4). He was concerned that they remain in Christ and not be distracted by the law or religion. If they turned back to these, they would be deprived of all profit from Christ and so separated or severed from Him, making Him void of effect. To make circumcision a condition of salvation was to relinquish Christ, who would then profit them nothing.

In Ephesians Paul prayed that the Father would strengthen the believers "with power through His Spirit into the inner man, that Christ may make His home in your hearts through faith" (3:16-17). Our inner man has to be strengthened that Christ may make His home in our hearts. He has to occupy us to such an extent that our whole being becomes His home.

"To me to live is Christ" Paul tells us in Philippians 1:21. Christ was everything to him. In 3:8 he declares how precious this One was to him. "I count also all things to be loss on account of the excellency of the knowledge of Christ Jesus my Lord, on account of Whom I have suffered the loss of all things and count them refuse that I may gain Christ." Because of Christ's surpassing worth, Paul counted everything else loss in order to gain Him.

Colossians tells us further how great Christ is. "And He is the Head of the Body, the church; Who is the beginning, Firstborn from among the dead, that He might have the first place in all things" (1:18). He is all-inclusive, He is the reality of all positive things (2:17), He is now our life (3:4), and He is all and in all in the new man (3:11).

How great was the Christ that Paul saw! We all need such a vision in order to hold the Head.

DISTRACTED BY PROPHECY

When I was first saved, I loved the Lord and His Word. As a young man, I loved the Bible and made up my mind I would come to understand every verse of it. I would spend my whole life on this! Now I have learned that the Bible is too profound for me ever to fully grasp. At the beginning I thought I was progressing quite well in my efforts. I would hunt for books on the Bible and would go wherever the Bible was taught. Eventually I was caught by the Brethren. When I started going to their meetings, they were preaching on the seventy weeks in Daniel (9:24-27). In all my years in Christianity, from the time I was born, I had never heard of these seventy weeks. I was fascinated. Later on, I heard about ten toes, four beasts, and ten horns. I began to study these strange, yet very scriptural subjects. In the years I spent among the Brethren I do not recall ever hearing a message on Christ. One day I realized how poor my condition was. I had learned all about the prophecies, but I was dead. I was powerless. In my disappointment I turned. The Lord gave me a turn away from the ten toes, the ten horns, the four beasts, and the seventy weeks!

I turned to Christ, to the Spirit, to life, and to the church! Since 1932 my attention has been focused on these matters. In message after message these are the subjects you hear in the Lord's recovery. I must warn you young people not to be distracted from these to other things. You may be approached by some who will ask you what the meaning is of the seven seals, the seven trumpets, and the seven bowls. If you do not know, they will make you feel your knowledge of the Bible is too restricted, that you know only about Christ, the Spirit, life, and the church. Young people are eager for knowledge. If you are distracted by prophecy, you will not hold the Head. I do not mean that you should not study other things in the Bible. You should study them, but you must see that all these other things are minor. The major things in the Bible are Christ, the Spirit, life, and the church.

DISTRACTED BY DOCTRINES

It is easy to be distracted. I know of some who have been distracted to keeping the Sabbath. Instead of caring for Christ, the all-inclusive Spirit, the divine life, and the church, they talk about the seventh day. Others are distracted about the way of baptism. You may be asked by some preacher what kind of baptism the church practices: sprinkling or immersion, in what name, forwards or backwards, how many times. How would you answer? Will you be distracted? A sister who attended a Lord's table meeting in Los Angeles afterwards wrote me a letter objecting to our use of wine. How would you have answered her? I have spent quite some time studying whether wine or grape juice should be used for the Lord's table. There is something to be said on both sides. You cannot make a firm decision. What is the use, then, of arguing about such matters? Head coverings for the sisters is another question you may well be asked about. If you say you believe in head coverings, they may go on to ask what color, what shape, and what size. Turn away from all these distracting considerations!

My word to you is: hold the Head! Christianity is in thousands of divisions because of these distractions. When any such questions are presented to you, you can inwardly pray: "Lord, have mercy upon me. Help me to hold You as the Head. I don't want to be ensnared by these distracting questions. I would hold the Head."

When Paul wrote of "not holding the Head" in Colossians 2:19, he was referring to those who were distracting the church in Colossae with Judaism, Greek philosophy, and Gnosticism. It is only when you hold the Head that you are kept from such distractions and can correspond to the ministry of Christ in the heavens. As long as you hold the Head, you will grow. The reason so few Christians correspond to Christ's heavenly ministry is that they have been distracted from holding the Head.

Ephesians 4:14 says, "That we may be no longer babes tossed by waves and carried about by every wind of teaching in the sleight of men, in craftiness with a view to a system of error." The wind that carries the babes about is teaching. It is not a wind of heresy, but even proper, scriptural doctrine, which can carry us away—away from Christ, the Head, and away from the church, the Body. This wind is part of Satan's system to deceive the believers and lure them from Christ. How important it is to hold the Head and not allow any doctrine, however biblical, to distract us from Him!

GIVING THE LORD GROUND

As we hold the Head, we shall grow up into Him (Eph. 4:15). Gradually we shall see that, in one thing after another, we are not in Christ. As we see, we can pray, "Lord, take over. In this matter I give You the ground." This is the practical growth in life. We belong to Christ, but in many things we are not in Him. In those things He has no ground in us. In our way of talking, He may have no ground. As we hold the Head, we shall realize that our speaking is not in Christ. If we ask the Lord to take over in this area, we shall grow in life regarding our talking.

Many Christians love the Lord, but He does not have the

ground in them because they are not holding Christ. When they hold Him, the Spirit within may speak to them about their clothing. If they say, "Lord, I give You the ground to deal with my way of dressing," then He will come in and take over. The same may be true of the way a brother treats his wife or of a sister's attitude toward her husband. They may love the Lord, but in their marital relationship they will not give Him one inch. If they hold the Head, the Spirit within will tell them that Christ has no ground in their attitude. As they open and give the Lord the ground, He will occupy them more and more.

To thus give ground to the Lord in your daily life is the proper way to grow in life. You do not grow by gathering scriptural knowledge. To grow in life is to let the Lord take over in every practical matter. As you do this in matter after matter, attitude after attitude, you will grow in those particular areas. The Lord will gradually fill you and possess your whole being. Then you will mature. By this growth in life your function will emerge, and the Body will be built up. This is a deeper and finer correspondence to the Lord's heavenly ministry. It is by this means that the churches are being built up.

THE BUILDING UP OF THE BODY

May we all see that in God's economy nothing counts but Christ. We have been transferred into Him. He is our portion, our enjoyment, and our life. He is the life-giving Spirit. He is to be everything to us. Such a vision will preserve us. We shall not allow any doctrine to distract us; doctrines are like wild beasts waiting to devour us! We must hold the Head with fear and trembling. Then the Spirit day after day will keep speaking to us: "In this thing you still keep the ground for yourself. In that other thing you have never given in to the Lord. In this area you have not given the Lord an inch of ground. In that area you are still holding out."

If we are holding the Head, we shall respond, "Lord, in this I give You the ground. In that I open for You to take over." Such a response results in our growth in life. Christ increases in us by His being able to take more ground. Then our function will come forth, and the Body will be built up. This vital correspondence to the Lord's heavenly ministry is finer than the outward move in life to bring people into God's move. To correspond to Him in this deeper way makes possible the building up of His Body.

Chapter Seven

THE HEAVENLY PRIESTHOOD OF CHRIST

Scripture Reading: Heb. 2:17; 3:1; 4:14-16; 5:5-6, 10; 6:20; 7:27-28; 8:1; 10:21; Rom. 8:34

As you are probably aware, the Bible tells us that Christ has three offices: prophet, priest, and king. Christ came the first time mainly as the Prophet foretold in Deuteronomy 18:15, 18. In His earthly ministry He spoke for God, spoke forth God, taught the disciples, and prophesied. This was His role as prophet. Then in the last part of His earthly ministry He began to offer Himself to God until finally on the cross He offered Himself as the sacrifices to God for us. In this He was fulfilling His role as priest. From that point on, He has had this function.

THE EARTHLY PRIESTHOOD FULFILLED

In Levitical times the priests did two kinds of work. The first was the offering of sacrifices to God in the outer court around the altar. Once the offerings were made, the priests entered into the Holy Place. The high priest entered the Holy of Holies. Here they would minister to God on behalf of His people.

The first priestly work typifies Christ's earthly priesthood; the second, His heavenly. When Christ offered Himself on the cross to God for us, He was a priest, offering on the earth in the outer court. Then after His resurrection He entered into the third heaven, which is the Holy of Holies. Here He continues to serve as the heavenly priest. It is this second aspect of His priesthood that we shall consider now.

This priesthood in the heavens is what mostly occupies Christ today. It is a vast subject for us to cover. The book of

Hebrews deals with this matter quite comprehensively. Since we are limited by time in our consideration of it here, I recommend that you read the Life-study Messages on Hebrews that deal with it (especially Messages 13, 27, 28, 31, 32, 33, and 35).

OUR PRIEST BOTH HUMAN AND DIVINE

For Christ to be a priest, He must be a man (Heb. 2:16-17). The high priest was "taken from among men" (5:1). If he had been an angel, he would not have had any understanding of human problems. Because the priest was chosen from among men, he could sympathize with man's weakness. Our High Priest today, Jesus Christ, is a man! He has partaken of our nature. He has shared in blood and flesh. He has been made like us in all things. He had to eat and drink. Sometimes He even wept. He shed tears at the tomb of Lazarus (John 11:35); He wept over Jerusalem at the end of His earthly ministry (Luke 19:41); and He prayed "with strong crying and tears" (Heb. 5:7) in the garden of Gethsemane. Even today He is a man, a man in the glory. "For we do not have a high priest who is not able to sympathize with our weaknesses, but One Who has been tried in all respects like us, yet without sin" (Heb. 4:15). Because He thoroughly knows all our weak points and problems, He sympathizes with us. Such is our High Priest as a man.

Our High Priest is also God! Because He is human, He can sympathize with us. But because He is also divine, He can take care of us. In the Old Testament the high priest Aaron could sympathize with the people, but many times he could not help them, because he was not divine. Our High Priest, however, is according to the order not of Aaron but of Melchisedec (Heb. 5:6, 10; 6:20). Of Melchisedec no genealogy is recorded in Genesis (14:18-20) that he might be a proper type of Christ as the eternal One to be our High Priest perpetually. As a man, Christ knows our case and sympathizes with us; as God, He is able to take care of all our needs. Hallelujah for this God-man who is our High Priest!

The priesthood of Christ is "not according to the law of a fleshy commandment, but according to the power of an indestructible life" (Heb. 7:16). Aaron was constituted high priest according to the powerless letter of the law, but Christ according to the powerful element of an indestructible life. Our High Priest is constituted of a life which nothing can conquer, but which rather conquers everything! It is a life which cannot be destroyed. A life which saves to the uttermost. The endless, eternal, divine, uncreated life. The resurrection life which has passed the test of death and Hades.

Our High Priest is now serving God for us in the Holy of Holies. He is our Representative in the supreme court of the heavens! He is our Attorney, presenting our case to God. We do not fully realize how much Christ is doing for us there. Though His redemptive work has been accomplished, His heavenly service to us never ceases.

INTERCEDING FOR US IN OUR NEED

How much we need Him!

> I need Thee, oh, I need Thee;
> Every hour I need Thee.
> *Hymns,* #371

Surely every hour we need Him. From hour to hour we do not know what situations will confront us. We may say hallelujah or amen in the meeting, but when we get home, our joy may vanish, and instead of hallelujah and amen there will be silence and a long face. A problem has arisen. Or we may get chilled and catch cold. Whatever the problem, Christ is there taking care of our case. He bears us when we have a long face or are ill. His interceding never ceases. His ability to take care of us is unlimited because He is the almighty God. His priesthood is an interceding ministry in the heavens, in the Holy of Holies, before God for us.

You are often unaware of His interceding, but sometimes you do realize that He is thus caring for you. You may be in the midst of an argument with your wife, when suddenly your words fail. Why do the angry words no longer come tumbling out? Before you were saved, did you ever have such an experience? In my own case, I used to go into a rage that could last the whole day, even overnight. Since I have been saved, however, I have never been able to get fully angry. The most my anger has lasted, as far as I can recall, is a few minutes. How about your case? How long can you stay angry? Not very long, because Christ is there interceding for you at the throne of God, and His interceding is heard.

Sometimes troubles come to us, and we get anxious. Before we were saved, these worries were endless. Now, when anxious thoughts arise, we soon sense a soothing comfort, saying to us, "Why don't you pray? You don't need to worry." Christ has begun to intercede for us, and this is the effect it produces. Then we respond to Him, "Thank You, Lord. You bear my worries. All my cares are in Your hand." Just a few short words and the anxiety is lifted! We can enjoy Him. This is Christ's priestly intercession for us. It is unending.

In Romans 8:34 Paul asks, "Who is he that condemns? It is Christ Jesus Who died, but rather Who was raised, Who is even at the right hand of God, Who also intercedes for us." There is no one who can condemn us. Christ surely does not; He died for us, was resurrected, and is now in the heavens interceding for us. His heavenly ministry is to take care of us.

We have all had many experiences of our faithful High Priest's care for us. Many times we have been reminded, comforted, strengthened, and even carried by Him. If we had time, we could hear testimony after testimony of how the help has come, not so much from the outside as from within. The help comes also from the heavens. There is something within and something from above that strengthens, sustains, comforts, and enlightens us. Without this support from our High Priest's intercession, we would long since have been gone. We have been preserved not by ourselves, but by our High Priest.

Our High Priest is well qualified for His office. The book of Hebrews gives us His qualifications. He is the Son of God (1:5), the Son of Man (2:6-9), the Captain of our salvation (2:10), the Apostle sent from God to us (3:1), and the real Joshua bringing us into rest (4:8). This well-qualified One is now caring for us in every detail. His intercession is precious to the Father. God on the throne treasures the priesthood of His Son. So must we.

He is praying for you day and night. You may have been away from the Lord and the church life. You turned a deaf ear to everyone who tried to help you. But one day, perhaps while you were far away on a mountaintop, the thought came to you, Why not go back to the church? You were all by yourself, away from the influence of others, but still you heard this word within. How do you explain that? Surely it was the effect of Christ's priesthood. His intercession touched you while you were far off and brought you back.

We really do not need much help from the outside. We have a Helper in the heavenlies! Our help comes from the heavens to our spirit. Eventually the help comes from within. We have such a High Priest!

OUR CORRESPONDING TO THE HEAVENLY INTERCESSION

"Having therefore a great High Priest...let us come forward with boldness to the throne of grace" (Heb. 4:14-16). After picturing for us our High Priest caring for us in our weaknesses, the writer of Hebrews then exhorts us to come to the throne of grace. It is by thus coming forward that we correspond to His heavenly intercession.

Where is the throne of grace? We must answer that it is both in the heavens and in our spirit. If it were only in the heavens, how could we come to it? As our experience bears witness, the throne is also in our spirit. To illustrate, let us say that we have some anxiety. To be anxious is a characteristic of an intelligent person. Only those who are foolish are happy-go-lucky no matter what happens to them. If we are alert, thinking people, many things will cause us anxiety. When we are single, our thoughts are occupied with our own concerns. Once we are married, we have two people to worry about. Instead of thinking only of ourself, we shall be wondering about our spouse. What about that conversation we had last night? What about our future? What if one of us gets sick? We need a way to cope with all the troublesome thoughts and situations that come to us. Thank God that our spirit is connected to the Holy of Holies! When we turn from our mind to our spirit, we enter into the Holy of Holies. Once there, it is hard to figure out whether we are in heaven or on earth! The Holy of Holies has two ends, one in the heavens and the other in our spirit. Here in the Holy of Holies is the throne of grace.

What do we do at the throne of grace? We pray, worship, and look to the One on the throne. We praise and thank Him. From this throne flows the river of life. If we stay here a while, we shall have the sense that something from the throne of grace flows into us, through us, and out of us. We are experiencing the eternal life as the supplying grace. We receive mercy and "find grace for timely help" (Heb. 4:16). By coming to the throne of grace we are corresponding to Christ's heavenly priesthood. Whenever we turn to the spirit and come to the throne of grace, we correspond to His heavenly interceding. His interceding and our praying constitute a traffic between heaven and earth.

When the high priest entered the Holy of Holies, he bore on his shoulders the names of the twelve tribes (Exo. 28:6-10). These names were also inscribed on the breastplate (Exo. 28:21). Today our High Priest bears all of us before God in the heavenly Holy of Holies. He goes to God to bring us there and to bring our need to Him. In this Holy Place all our problems are solved. He is serving us at the throne of grace. Let us therefore come forward with boldness, that we may receive mercy and may find grace for timely help!

The throne of grace is the only place where our problems can be solved. As we come, we are corresponding from our side to the intercession on His side. This communication goes on all day long. Though none of this can be seen with our physical eyes, our spirit senses that something is going on in the Holy of Holies for us. Come to the throne of grace!

This office of High Priest is the greatest part of Christ's heavenly ministry. We are meeting Him there at the throne of grace, hour after hour enjoying, experiencing, and touching Him. As He intercedes for us, we are coming boldly to the throne to receive mercy and to find grace. These are always available to us. However, we need to receive and find them by exercising our spirit to come to the throne and to touch our High Priest, who sympathizes with us in all our weaknesses.

THE GREATNESS OF OUR HIGH PRIEST

How great is our High Priest! "He is able to save to the uttermost those who come forward to God through Him, seeing He is always living to intercede for them" (Heb. 7:25). The high priests who served under the law had weakness, so that they had to offer up sacrifices first for their own sins, and then for the sins of the people (v. 27). Our High Priest, in contrast, is "holy, guileless, undefiled, separated from sinners, and become higher than the heavens" (v. 26). He has no need to offer up sacrifices, "for this He did once for all when He offered up Himself" (v. 27). Rather than the weak men who served as high priests under the law, our High Priest is a "Son, Who is perfected forever" (v. 28). "We have such a High Priest, Who sat down on the right hand of the throne of the Majesty in the heavens" (8:1). He is the great Priest over the house of God (10:21).

CHAPTER EIGHT

CHRIST'S EXECUTION OF THE NEW TESTAMENT

Scripture Reading: Heb. 7:16, 25; 9:11-12, 15-17

In Hebrews 7 through 10 Christ is presented in a threefold way: as High Priest, as Minister, and as Executor of the new testament. When Christ is mentioned as the High Priest, we are also told that He is the Minister of the holy places and the Executor of the new testament. These three titles are mentioned together because their functions overlap. While Christ is carrying on His priestly work, He is also executing the new testament and simultaneously ministering its contents to us.

In this message we shall consider how He executes the new testament. This is the most complicated point in the New Testament for us to understand, yet it is all-inclusive.

GOD'S SPEAKING TO MAN

Throughout the Bible God's speaking was in three ways: His word, His promise, and His covenant (or testament). In God's speaking there was His promise. When His promise was enacted by an oath, it became a covenant, which is also a testament.

From the very beginning God spoke to man. Before Adam disobeyed, God spoke to him. After the fall God came again to speak to him, this time promising that the seed of the woman would bruise the head of the serpent (Gen. 3:15). With God's speaking came God's promise.

The same was true with Abraham. In God's speaking to him, He promised him a seed and the good land (Gen. 13:15). God spoke and God promised.

How did the promise become a covenant? It was by the addition of an oath with a sacrifice where blood was shed (e.g., Gen. 15:7-18). A covenant is an agreement in which one party promises certain things to the other party.

A testament, in turn, is a bequest of what has already been accomplished. In modern terms it is a will, a written legal statement for the distribution of the enactor's property upon his death. The entire Bible is actually God's testament; its two parts are even called the Old Testament and the New Testament.

God is a speaking God. The more He speaks the more He is bound by His words. But He cannot help but speak! He has much to say to man. The Bible is full of God's speaking. This book is God's word to man.

When we speak, we may unconsciously make promises. If we get others to talk to us, we may be able to induce them to promise us something they had no intention of promising. As long as they are quiet, we cannot ensnare them; but when they speak, we may be able to get a commitment from them.

God has spoken. In both the Old and New Testaments He has spoken. In His speaking He has made promises. The Bible is full of promises. Promises to Adam. To Noah. To Abraham. To David. To us, the New Testament believers.

If the Lord Jesus had not died, these promises would have remained only promises. But to fulfill these promises He did die. By the shedding of His blood these promises became a covenant. Now there is a firm commitment for them to be realized. In this covenant some things are yet to be done, and some have been accomplished already and have been bequeathed to us. The covenant then has become a testament, telling us what our inheritance is.

"And because of this He is Mediator of a new covenant, so that, death having taken place for redemption of the transgressions under the first covenant, those who have been called might receive the promise of the eternal inheritance. For where there is a testament there must of necessity be the death of him who made it. For a testament is confirmed where there has been death, since it has no force when he who made it is living" (Heb. 9:15-17).

In Greek the same word is used for both covenant and testament. The new covenant, consummated with the blood of

Christ (Heb. 9:11-14), is not merely a covenant, but a testament with all the things which have been accomplished by the death of Christ bequeathed to us. Firstly God gave the promise that He would make a new covenant (Jer. 31:31-34; Heb. 8:8-13). Then Christ shed His blood to enact it (Luke 22:20). Since there are accomplished facts promised in this covenant, it is also a testament. This testament, or will, has been confirmed and validated by Christ's death, and is being executed and enforced by Christ in His resurrection. The promise of God's covenant is insured by God's faithfulness; God's covenant is guaranteed by God's righteousness; and the testament is enforced by Christ's resurrection power.

The Bible first *tells* us that Christ will come. Then it *promises* us that He will come. There is not only the speaking but the promise as well. Many blessings are included in this promise. He will die for us that our sins might be forgiven and that we might be redeemed. Life will be given to us. This life is the Spirit, who is God Himself as everything to us for our enjoyment. Finally, we shall inherit whatever God is, whatever He has, and whatever He does.

After God's speaking and His promising (including the content of His promise), Christ went to the cross and died, shedding His blood. Because of His death, the promise has been consummated, the covenant has been established, and the testament has been enacted.

We have, then, four stages in God's speaking to man: His speaking, His promising, His covenant-making, and His testament-executing. Adam in Genesis 2 was in the first stage. Abraham in Genesis 12 was in the second, or promising, stage. The disciples, when they saw Christ dying on the cross, were in the third, the covenant-making, stage. We today are in the fourth stage, when the testament is executed. God has spoken, He has promised, Christ has made the covenant, and the covenant has become a testament to us.

OUR BEQUEST

We have already covered three aspects of Christ's heavenly ministry: how He exercises His rulership over the whole world that His gospel may be preached and God's called people be brought in; how He exercises His headship to cause us to grow and function that His Body may be built up; and how He intercedes for us and cares for us as our High Priest. In this message we shall consider the fourth aspect: how He executes the testament He has bequeathed to us. By the execution of the new testament by the heavenly Christ, He is making all the items listed therein real to us.

We all like to be remembered in someone's will. I am sure that all my children, and even my grandchildren, are expecting to be included in my will! Suppose we were willed a large piece of property with a mansion containing twenty-four rooms and seven bathrooms and, in addition, ten million German marks. We would surely be pleased! However, we would need to make sure that the inheritance was more than just two items written on paper. The will would have to be executed in order for us to come into possession of what we had been bequeathed.

Have you ever tried to find out what is included in the new testament? It is a long list! In fact, after trying many times to enumerate all the items, I have concluded that it cannot be done. The list is endless. Here are some of the items: redemption, forgiveness of sins, justification, reconciliation, regeneration, sanctification, sonship, life, power, peace, holiness, etc.

Have you received all these bequests? Sometimes the heir is young and does not realize what he has inherited. Or perhaps the heir is simple and cannot understand the meaning of the terms in the will. Or in a third case, the heir may be too weak to lay claim to his inheritance, even though he is mature and wise. In all these cases, someone is needed to help the intended heir gain possession of what has been bequeathed to him.

THE COVENANT ENACTED BY THE BLOOD OF CHRIST

When Christ died on the cross, He made God's promise a covenant. His blood was the enacting symbol. The Lord's table, which we have week by week, is a symbol of the will. The Lord took the cup and gave thanks. Then He gave it to the disciples, saying, "Drink of it, all of you; for this is My blood of the covenant, which is poured out for many for forgiveness of sins" (Matt. 26:27-28). The words in Luke 22:20 are: "This cup is the new testament in my blood, which is shed for you." The cup that we take is the new covenant. This is a profound fact. When we take the cup, we need to realize that it is the new covenant.

The two main items in the new covenant are the forgiveness of sins and the impartation of life. By these we enjoy God. He is the blessing of the cup. He is the eternal portion of its blessing.

The blood of Jesus, then, enacted the covenant. His death confirmed it. Then in resurrection He comes to execute its contents.

THE TESTAMENT EXECUTED

He is now in the heavens, living, divine, capable, constituted of the indestructible life. Nothing can thwart Him! Nothing can destroy Him! He is the living One, living forever! Thus, He is able to execute this testament in every detail.

Do you need life? power? forgiveness? peace? holiness? Of course, your needs are many. How can you be supplied? In the testament are all these items. They are bequeathed to you. Christ today is executing the testament, making every item available and real to you.

Suppose your wife gives you a hard time. You need patience. Where can you find the patience to endure being under her thumb? Patience is one of the items listed in the will. It is applied and made real to you by Christ's execution. When patience is your need, He will make it available to you. You will have the sense that patience comes into you like a flood. Is this not your experience?

The same is true of joy. You may be suffering, but there is joy in this will. How can that joy be real to you? Christ Himself will execute joy into you, flooding you with it.

You may wonder how I can have so much to speak. You may think I will run out of things to say. Included in this will, though, is the rich Word. When I am to give a message, I do not turn to reference books to find a subject, to put together some points, to study some commentaries, and to thus organize what I shall say. No! Christ as the Executor floods the riches of God's Word into me. Out of this flood comes the rich thought, the rich utterances. Thus the speaking is endless.

What a will we have! What an Executor—living, powerful, capable!

Christ's intercession is part of the execution of the will. You may be short of life and light. You may not be enjoying God as your life and light. Your High Priest will then pray for you, that you may have the rich enjoyment of God. This is His intercession. Then He will exercise His position to execute the life and light from God into you. This is the answer to His intercession and also the enforcement of His will.

OUR CORRESPONDENCE

Just as you need the proper correspondence to His intercession by coming to the throne of grace, so you also need the proper corresponding to His executing of the will. You have been lacking in this corresponding because of not being helped to see these matters. Probably you have never before heard such messages. From now on, there is no reason to be off; you can correspond to Him!

Hebrews 7:25 gives us the way to correspond to His executing of the new covenant: "Wherefore also He is able to save to the uttermost those who come forward to God through Him, seeing He is always living to intercede for them." We cooperate with Him by coming forward to God.

Keep coming forward to God. Morning and evening, day and night, while you are praying and when you are not, come forward to Him! "O God, I am open to You. You are rich. I need You. I need all there is for me in Your will. I want to stay open to You all the time." As you do this, Christ the able One will execute into your being whatever you need. It is part of His heavenly ministry to thus execute item after item from the will into you for your enjoyment.

To realize this will be a strengthening to you. Suppose your working day is over and you are ready to go home. You have put in eight hours of hard work, and you are tired. But the thought of going home is not very appealing, because you never know what situation will confront you. Whether you will be greeted by a long face or a smiling face you cannot predict. Some days when you go home, you encounter a storm. Other days it is calm and sunny. You cannot bear to walk into a storm tonight. What should you do? Do not forget the will! Open yourself. Come forward to God. You may only say, "O God my Father, I am opening myself to You," and you will have the deep conviction that you are strengthened. He has interceded for you. He has also executed something into you. You are strengthened into the inner man. Now you are ready to go home. You can declare, "Lord, whether the weather is wild or mild doesn't matter to me. I want to go back home and enjoy You. It may be under a clear sky or a cloudy sky. Rain or shine, I will still be opening to You. You will be my supply, according to Your will. I am included in Your will. Father, that will binds You. Moreover, I have an Executor, who is seeing to it that I get all the items listed in that will. My circumstances don't bother me. Your will makes every provision for me."

Christ's heavenly ministry is not over. His earthly ministry has indeed been accomplished. But as the Executor of the new covenant, He is still ministering to strengthen, comfort, supply, sustain, and even bear you. His purpose in so doing is that you may grow and function that His Body may be built up. His heavenly ministry, the goal of which is the building up of His Body, has many different aspects. We have already considered four of them. There is the exercise of His rulership, the exercise of His headship, the priesthood, and the execution of God's will and testament. In the next message we shall go on to another aspect.

CHAPTER NINE

THE MORE EXCELLENT MINISTRY OF CHRIST IN THE TRUE TABERNACLE

Scripture Reading: Heb. 8:1-2, 6; 9:15-17

THE WILL AND THE EXECUTOR

We have a marvelous testament and a wonderful Executor! The testament is actually the whole Bible. It began as God's speaking. Then it became His promise. Later it became His covenant. Now that everything has been accomplished through Christ's death, it is a testament or will, with every item of its content bequeathed to us. All the things in this will are ours.

We have a wonderful Executor to see that this will is carried out! He is God, yet He became a man. He lived on this earth and tasted all the sufferings of human life. At the end of His experience of human living, He died on the cross. By this means He dealt with our sins, overcame Satan, terminated the whole old creation, and solved all the problems. He satisfied God and met all His requirements. After three days of rest, He came forth from death and entered into resurrection. In resurrection He has uplifted humanity and has Himself become a life-giving Spirit. This is the compound, all-inclusive Spirit. This wonderful Person—God and man, dead and resurrected, living forever, strong and capable—is executing whatever is in this will for our benefit and enjoyment.

How privileged we are to live in the stage when the will is in effect and to have such a capable Executor to enforce all its provisions for us to enjoy!

THE MINISTRY OF MELCHISEDEC

The book of Hebrews tells us that Christ is High Priest, not according to the order of Aaron, but according to the order of Melchisedec (7:11-17). At the end of His human living on this earth, He acted as High Priest, offering Himself as a sacrifice to God. This earthly part of His priesthood—to offer the sacrifice for the accomplishment of redemption—was typified by Aaron, the high priest chosen by God from among His people. Now that this has been accomplished, Christ in resurrection is the heavenly High Priest, according to the order of Melchisedec.

What is our heavenly Melchisedec doing? He is no longer offering sacrifices; He is now the serving One. As a minister is a serving one, supplying those he serves with what they need, so this Minister provides us with the heavenly supply, ministering God Himself into us.

In the account in Genesis 14:18-20, when Abraham returned from the slaughter of the kings, Melchisedec, priest of the most high God, came out to meet him with bread and wine. Melchisedec was not an offering high priest, but rather a serving priest. Abraham must have been weary after battling with the kings. In his exhaustion he surely needed a supply. Christ is now doing in the heavenlies what Melchisedec did for Abraham: He serves us with a life supply for our need. There is no need for any more sacrifices; His one offering satisfied God forever (Heb. 10:12).

Christ's heavenly priesthood is to serve us with bread and wine. Christ is also a "Minister of the holy places, even of the true tabernacle, which the Lord pitched, not man" (Heb. 8:2). The true tabernacle is the heavenly Holy of Holies, where Jesus has entered within the veil as our High Priest (6:19-20). Besides being the High Priest interceding for us and the Mediator executing the new testament, our Christ is Intercessor, Executor, and Minister! We have such a High Priest!

THE TESTAMENT AS OUR GROUND

This service is based upon the testament. It is not groundless, but rather firmly based. Suppose, as an illustration, there is a bank with plenty of money. I have no cash in my pocket, so I go there to get some money. Unfortunately I have no account there, or my account has insufficient funds. My request for money has no ground. Suppose, instead, someone has deposited ten million dollars in this bank. If I go to the bank and show his signature over a request for me to be given the money, I shall have the ground to request money from his account.

All too often we approach God in our need and beg for His mercy. We shed tears and pray, "Father, how I need Your mercy! Do have mercy on me in my sad condition. I thank You that You are the merciful God." Beseeching in this way is like going to the bank and saying to the manager, "Oh, do have mercy upon me! I am desperately in need of money. Pity me, and let me have some money to meet my bills." Would it not be foolish to use this approach to get money from a bank? We have no ground if we plead in this way.

What is the ground on which we make our requests known to God? It is the will, the very testament which Christ has enacted and bequeathed to us. On this ground Christ is carrying out His heavenly priesthood and interceding in the heavens. We need this Executor to interrupt our begging prayers and remind us, "Why are you praying in such a pitiful way? Come to the throne boldly! Come to the bank and claim your money! Here is the will. I am your Executor. You may be young and foolish, but I am your Attorney. Who would dare cheat you? I am the Son of God, the One who died on the cross for you and who is now living in resurrection!"

How do you handle the day-to-day troubles that beset you? I am afraid that especially the sisters shed their tears and groan to the Lord. You forget the testament and the Executor. The Bible and Christ are far off. Only your tears are nearby. I have the same tendency myself. I do not shed tears, but sometimes I wonder what to do when trouble arises. Then I remember that I must look to the Lord. I call, "O Lord Jesus! Have mercy on me!" He truly is merciful! While I am calling on Him, He reminds me of the testament and of His position as my Executor and Attorney. How many times He has reminded me! Then I realize afresh that the Son of the living

God, the very Christ in resurrection, is taking sides with me, is standing with me, is interceding for me, and is executing His will for me. I am strengthened. I turn from my anxiety and praise Him. Sisters, save your tears. Praise Him instead for executing the will for you.

How blessed we are to be in the Lord's recovery! What we have heard is foreign to the ears of many of those outside. When we were in Christianity, we may have heard about Daniel's seventy weeks, the ten horns, and the four beasts. But very little, if anything, came to us about the testament as our bequest and the living Christ as the Executor. We have seen what others have not seen. Now we are enjoying what many others have not had a way to enjoy. We do not realize how much we have been blessed.

THE SUPPLYING MINISTER

After the interceding and the executing of the will, this very Intercessor and Executor is the Minister, bringing us whatever it is that we need and serving it to us. Here on earth I may be having trouble upon trouble. My situation causes me worry and anxiety. I cannot see any way out. This may be my case on earth. But, hallelujah, a different situation prevails in the heavens!

There the High Priest is interceding for me. The Executor is carrying out the provisions of the will. In addition, the Minister picks up the very peace I need and supplies it to me. This peace was promised to me in John 14:27: "Peace I leave with you; My peace I give to you." It was promised also in Philippians 4:7: "The peace of God, which surpasses all understanding, will guard your hearts and your thoughts in Christ Jesus."

When troubles come, however, I forget these promises, which have become bequests, and remember only my worries. I forget all about what has been bequeathed to me, but He does not. He comes as the life-giving Spirit indwelling my spirit. He comes as the heavenly Melchisedec, this time bringing not bread and wine, but peace. This One comes to visit me. Within me, for no observable reason, I am suddenly filled with peace. The worry is gone. The anxiety has vanished. How has this change come about? I have experienced Christ's heavenly ministry as the High Priest, as the Executor, and as the Minister.

No doubt you too have had experiences like this. In the past, however, you did not understand them. Now the light and knowledge have come to you. No trial should overcome you. You have a High Priest interceding for you. You have One executing the provisions of His will on your behalf. And you have a Servant supplying you with the right thing at the right time. In every situation that arises, this heavenly ministry is acting on your behalf. After many experiences of His care, you will gradually realize that there is no need for you to worry. Christ is there ministering in the heavens for you!

Christ is interchangeably called High Priest, Minister, and Mediator in Hebrews (8:1, 2, 6; 9:11, 15). The High Priest is the Minister, and the Minister is the Mediator. The term Executor is not explicitly used, but it is implied in chapter nine. "He is Mediator of a new covenant, so that, death having taken place for redemption of the transgressions under the first covenant, those who have been called might receive the promise of the eternal inheritance. For where there is a testament there must of necessity be the death of him who made it. For a testament is confirmed where there has been death, since it has no force when he who made it is living" (9:15-17). Christ in His death enacted the new covenant and bequeathed it to us as the new testament. After death He entered into resurrection and became the One to enforce the new testament. These four titles—High Priest, Minister, Mediator, and Executor—all refer to Christ in resurrection.

IN THE HEAVENS AND WITHIN

This very Christ is now the Lord in the heavens and at the same time the Spirit within us. "Now the Lord is the Spirit" (2 Cor. 3:17). As Lord, He is in the heavens. As the Spirit, He is within us. As the One in the heavens, He is exercising His rulership, headship, and priesthood. He exercises His rulership for the spreading of the gospel, that God's chosen people may be brought in. He exercises His headship to cause all His members to grow and function, that His Body might be built up. He exercises His priesthood to rescue us from all our troublesome entanglements by interceding, by executing the provisions of the new testament, and by serving us whatever we need; this is how He keeps us from falling. All these are His activities as Lord in the heavens.

Whatever He carries out as Lord, He applies to us as the Spirit. How are all His heavenly functions to be realized by us? Whatever He intercedes, or executes, or ministers, is transmitted into our spirit. As the Lord in the heavens, He is the electricity in the power plant; as the Spirit in our spirit, He is the electricity in this building. The Lord in the heavens and the Spirit in our spirit are one. There is a continual transmission between the heavens and our spirit, so that whatever transpires there is immediately applied here.

Notice that this traffic is between the heavens and our spirit. Our mind does not count. It is our mind that causes us to worry. When the heavenly transmission comes, the wonderful reality strengthens our spirit. Then our spirit rises to shout, "Praise the Lord!" The transmission has come to our spirit, not to our mind. The Spirit in our spirit is the very One who is Lord in the heavens.

Romans 8 confirms that the One who is the Spirit is the very One who is the Lord. Verse 26 tells us that "the Spirit Himself intercedes for us with groanings which cannot be uttered." Then verse 34 says that Christ Jesus "is even at the right hand of God, Who also intercedes for us." Who is interceding for us? It is the Lord Spirit! In the heavens it is the Lord; in us it is the Spirit. The same is true of Melchisedec. There is only one Melchisedec. In the heavens He is the Lord; in our spirit He is the Spirit. Doctrinally, we have no satisfactory explanation for this twofold reality; from our experience, however, we do have the confirmation.

You may be coming back from work exhausted, wondering how you will find things at home. Unexpectedly, while you are thinking, you sense that you are supplied and strengthened. What is the source of this supply? It has come from the very Christ who is both Lord in the heavens and the Spirit within us. He is interceding for you, caring for you, and executing the new testament for you. Based upon this testament,

He picks up the life supply and comes to support you with the very thing you need. You experience Him as Lord, Spirit, High Priest, Executor, and Minister. He is also the Mediator, transmitting what you need from God the Father, who is the source, into your spirit to supply and support you.

THE SUSTAINING PRIEST

Surely we have all experienced this heavenly ministry of Christ. How is it that we have been kept from falling all these years? I can testify that this is what has preserved me for over fifty-five years. In His earthly ministry, He died for me on the cross. Now He is serving me in resurrection; this is His heavenly ministry. Its main element is the priesthood for the members of His Body. Of course, He did exercise His rulership to see that I was saved and thus brought to God. He also exercised His headship over me to cause me to grow and function and so be built up in His Body. But mostly it has been His priesthood which He has exercised again and again to preserve me. Hallelujah for our heavenly High Priest! We have been sustained, preserved, and supplied by His interceding, His executing the testament, and His ministering to us what we have needed. I have had no lack. A rich life supply has been my portion.

His preserving and sustaining of us are fully wrapped up with His priesthood, which is based upon the will. The will is in our hand, and this High Priest is both in the heavens and in us. In the heavens He is the Lord. In us He is the Spirit. This Lord Spirit constantly ministers the life supply to us. The supply that comes to us is heavenly, because heaven is its source. Our High Priest is ministering to us in the true tabernacle, the heavenly Holy of Holies, which is joined to our spirit by Him as the heavenly ladder (Gen. 28:12; John 1:51). By His ministering to us the heavenly supply, He is making us a heavenly people. We are a people on this earth living a heavenly life.

CHAPTER TEN

THE UNIVERSAL ADMINISTRATION OF CHRIST IN THE HEAVENS

Scripture Reading: Rev. 1:11-13, 16-18, 20; 2:1; 3:1; 21; 5:1-10; 7:2-3; 8:3-5; 10:1-2; 18:1; 20:4, 6; 22:1, 3

In our previous messages we have seen that Christ is now exercising His rulership for the spread of the gospel, that His people might be brought in; He is exercising His headship to cause us to grow and function, that His Body might be built up; He is exercising His priesthood to intercede for us; He is executing the new testament for us; and He is ministering the life supply to us. We are well taken care of. As far as we are concerned, there is no shortage. But how about the universe? How about God's whole purpose? For this, we need to consider one further aspect of the Lord's ministry in the heavens.

This final aspect, of Christ's universal administration in the heavens, is unfolded for us in the book of Revelation. The whole universe, both the heavens and the earth, is under His authority. He is the universal Administrator.

THE HIGH PRIEST CARING FOR THE CHURCHES

In Revelation we first see that Christ, God's anointed One, is now caring for His church. He is caring for it in an administrative way. The churches are God's lampstands shining forth His testimony. They need Christ's administration. Sometimes troubles and difficulties arise, requiring His administrative attention. In the ancient time the high priest took care of the lampstand, seeing that all the lamps were trimmed so they would keep shining brightly. Our High Priest today is doing this very same work as He walks in the midst of the lampstands (Rev. 1:11-13).

He is further caring for the churches by holding all the responsible ones in His hand. The leading ones in the churches are likened to stars, shining in the heavens during the darkness of the night (Rev. 1:16, 20). We who are the serving ones need to be aware that we are not in our own hands, but His. He administrates the lampstands and holds the stars. The view given us in Revelation 1 shows us how the local churches in this age can go on. The situation among Christians is surely disappointing and discouraging. We must turn away from the earthly view and look to Christ! He is the First and the Last! He is the living One, even living forever! He is able! He it is who is now holding "the seven stars in His right hand" and walking "in the midst of the seven golden lampstands" (2:1). He "opens and no one shall shut, and shuts and no one shall open" (3:7). By looking away to Him we shall be encouraged. The local churches will never fail because of this Administrator walking among us, holding the leading ones!

Such is Christ's administration in the churches.

THE REDEEMING LAMB EXECUTING THE TESTAMENT

The book of Revelation also tells us that Christ is the Administrator taking care of all peoples. There are the Jews, God's elect; the heathen, the nations; and those in Christendom. We need to be aware that even Christendom and how it will progress are under Christ's administration. When all these categories of people have been dealt with according to Christ's rule, there will be the millennium, the kingdom of God on this earth. Afterwards there will be a new age, eternity, with the New Jerusalem and the new heaven and the new earth. Of these peoples and ages Christ is the Administrator.

This is what is unfolded to us, beginning with Revelation 4. The scene changes from Christ's tending of the lampstands (chapters one to three) to "a door opened in heaven," and we are shown "what must take place after these things" (4:1). Christ is presented as the redeeming Lamb who is the Victor, qualified to take up the new testament, open it, and execute it. Such is the meaning of the sealed scroll in the right hand

THE UNIVERSAL ADMINISTRATION OF CHRIST

of the One on the throne (5:1). When a strong angel calls out, "Who is worthy to open the scroll and to break its seals?" (5:2), only this worthy Lion-Lamb is able to come and take the scroll (5:5-7). He is qualified to take the new testament, open it, and execute it.

The new testament in the Epistles of Paul is mainly for our enjoyment of the riches of Christ which have been bequeathed to us. There is, however, another aspect to the new testament. God deals with the universe according to His testament. How He deals with the Jews, the nations, and Christendom will all be according to His testament. In this testament are bequests for us as believers to enjoy. In this testament are also the matters of God's dealing with different peoples and even with the heavens and the earth. This new testament the Redeemer of the whole universe is qualified to take, open, and execute.

Eventually everything in the universe will be headed up in Christ. The Jews, the heathen nations, and Christendom will all be dealt with, and God's kingdom ushered in on this earth. When all things are headed up in Christ, there will be the fullness of the times. The heavens will be new. So will the earth and everything in it. The whole universe will be in order. There will be no more division, confusion, darkness, death, night, nor tears.

When people ask us how we are, we usually reply "fine." Actually, everything is not fine. Things are mixed up, confused, dark, and under death. There is reason to shed tears. Even the men should shed tears for the pitiful state of things. To say that we are fine or that things are fine is not true. No one is fine. No family is fine. No society is fine.

A day will come, however, when there will be a new heaven and a new earth. All things will be headed up in Christ. Everything will be in order. Then everything will be fine. Who is worthy to administrate this new heaven and new earth with the New Jerusalem? Only Christ. He is the One who died to redeem the whole universe. He is the One who conquered Satan through His death. He is the One who consummated the covenant with His redeeming blood. He is the One who bequeathed the new testament to us.

How qualified He is! He is worthy to take up the scroll of

the new testament, open it up, execute all that is written therein, provide us with every bequest, carry out every item contained in it, and bring everything in the universe into order. This is Christ's ultimate heavenly ministry, the carrying out of all that God designed.

"ANOTHER ANGEL"

In Revelation Christ is first presented as the High Priest for the churches. He walks in their midst, taking care of their shining and holding all the leading ones in His hand, that the churches may go on, even in the dark night of a degraded situation.

Christ is next portrayed as the overcoming Lamb, the Lion-Lamb qualified to execute the new testament.

Then in chapters seven, eight, ten, and eighteen, He is referred to as "another Angel." That this title of "another Angel" refers to Christ is clear from the context. God has sent forth many angels, but Christ as God's sent One is extraordinary. In this role He is called another Angel.

Controlling the Universe

In chapter seven Christ as God's Angel controls the whole universe, directing the other angels to carry out God's judgment upon the earth (7:2-3).

Offering Prayers and Pouring Out the Answers

In chapter eight Christ is again depicted as another Angel, offering the prayers of the saints to God (8:3-5). For His administration He needs our prayers. Our prayer is the response to His heavenly ministry. As we pray, He administrates. As He administrates, we are praying. These prayers He offers to God, then pours out God's answers to them on this earth. This is the meaning of verse 5: "And the Angel took the censer and filled it with the fire of the altar and cast it to the earth; and there were thunders and voices and lightnings and an earthquake." The pouring out of God's answers to our prayers is equivalent to His universal administration. This Administrator is qualified in every way, yet He needs our prayers. We may say that Christ is administrating this whole universe through our prayers.

Possessing the Earth

In chapter ten another strong Angel is seen "coming down out of heaven, clothed with a cloud; and the rainbow was upon His head, and His face was as the sun, and His feet as pillars of fire...And He placed His right foot on the sea and the left on the land" (10:1-2). Here Christ as another Angel has left the throne in the heavens and is on the way back to earth. That He is clothed with a cloud indicates that at this stage His coming is secret. He is secretly on His way back to earth to possess it in its entirety. His one foot on the sea and the other on earth symbolizes His taking possession. The earth is the Lord's. It must all be His inheritance. He will come in power to take possession of it.

Judging Babylon

In 18:1 we are told: "After these things I saw another Angel coming down out of heaven, having great authority; and the earth was illumined with His glory." No longer is He enveloped by a cloud. He is out in the open and very close to earth. He comes to exercise His authority over Christendom, the Great Babylon. After thoroughly judging this evil religion, He will overcome Satan and establish the millennial kingdom on earth.

RULER IN THE KINGDOM AND FOR ETERNITY

In that kingdom He will rule, with all His overcomers as co-kings (Rev. 3:21; 20:4, 6). He will be the head Administrator of the kingdom. After those thousand years there will be the New Jerusalem, with its center the throne of God and of the Lamb (Rev. 22:1, 3). There the redeeming Lamb will be the Ruler for eternity. Even for eternity He is the Administrator. This universal administration is a great part of Christ's heavenly ministry.

FULFILLMENT THROUGH
THE CORRESPONDING MINISTRIES ON EARTH

Without Paul's completing ministry, Christ has no way to

carry out His heavenly ministry. The two correspond to each other. One is in the heavens, the other among the saints on this earth. Today we are under these two ministries. Even now Christ is ministering in the heavens, and Paul's completing ministry is being carried out here among us.

This completing ministry is carrying out God's economy to prepare a Body for Christ. The Head needs a Body. Consider what you could accomplish if you had only a head but no body. You could do nothing! Without the church, His Body, Christ can do nothing. The completing ministry, then, is to bring forth the Body so that the Head can carry out God's administration on earth.

Paul's completing ministry, as we shall see further in the upcoming messages, focuses upon Christ as the center of God's economy and the circumference of God's purpose. This Christ must live in us, and we must live Him. He is the all-inclusive One.

Then there is the wonderful church life! God has passed through a process to become the life-giving Spirit and to enter into our spirit. These two spirits become one when we are regenerated. From this point on, this all-inclusive Spirit would spread from within our spirit into our soul, that it might be saturated with the Triune God. This spreading of God within us is called transformation and the growth in life. By means of this growth, we are fitted together to be one Body. This Body is built up, not by teaching or arranging or going through formalities, but by the transformation of our soul. Then we grow together, not only as the Body, but also as the universal new man. Christ has His Body, and God has a new man. Then Christ can act, and God can carry out His eternal purpose.

This is the way in which Paul's completing ministry carries out Christ's heavenly ministry. After the series on the completing ministry of Paul, we shall continue with the mending ministry of John. With these three ministries the Bible is consummated, and the new heaven and earth with the New Jerusalem are brought in.

About the Author

Witness Lee was born in 1905 in northern China and raised in a Christian family. At age 19 he was fully captured for Christ and immediately consecrated himself to preach the gospel for the rest of his life. Early in his service, he met Watchman Nee, a renowned preacher, teacher, and writer. Witness Lee labored together with Watchman Nee under his direction. In 1934 Watchman Nee entrusted Witness Lee with the responsibility for his publication operation, called the Shanghai Gospel Bookroom.

Prior to the Communist takeover in 1949, Witness Lee was sent by Watchman Nee and his other co-workers to Taiwan to ensure that the things delivered to them by the Lord would not be lost. Watchman Nee instructed Witness Lee to continue the former's publishing operation abroad as the Taiwan Gospel Bookroom, which has been publicly recognized as the publisher of Watchman Nee's works outside China. Witness Lee's work in Taiwan manifested the Lord's abundant blessing. From a mere 350 believers, newly fled from the mainland, the churches in Taiwan grew to 20,000 in five years.

In 1962 Witness Lee felt led of the Lord to come to the United States, settling in California. During his 35 years of service in the U.S., he ministered in weekly meetings and weekend conferences, delivering several thousand spoken messages. Much of his speaking has since been published as over 400 titles. Many of these have been translated into over fourteen languages. He gave his last public conference in February 1997 at the age of 91.

He leaves behind a prolific presentation of the truth in the Bible. His major work, *Life-study of the Bible,* comprises over 25,000 pages of commentary on every book of the Bible from the perspective of the believers' enjoyment and experience of God's divine life in Christ through the Holy Spirit. Witness Lee was the chief editor of a new translation of the New Testament into Chinese called the Recovery Version and directed the translation of the same into English. The Recovery Version also appears in a number of other languages. He provided an extensive body of footnotes, outlines, and spiritual cross references. A radio broadcast of his messages can be heard on Christian radio stations in the United States. In 1965 Witness Lee founded Living Stream Ministry, a non-profit corporation, located in Anaheim, California, which officially presents his and Watchman Nee's ministry.

Witness Lee's ministry emphasizes the experience of Christ as life and the practical oneness of the believers as the Body of Christ. Stressing the importance of attending to both these matters, he led the churches under his care to grow in Christian life and function. He was unbending in his conviction that God's goal is not narrow sectarianism but the Body of Christ. In time, believers began to meet simply as the church in their localities in response to this conviction. In recent years a number of new churches have been raised up in Russia and in many eastern European countries.

OTHER BOOKS PUBLISHED BY
Living Stream Ministry

Titles by Witness Lee:

Abraham—Called by God	0-7363-0359-6
The Experience of Life	0-87083-417-7
The Knowledge of Life	0-87083-419-3
The Tree of Life	0-87083-300-6
The Economy of God	0-87083-415-0
The Divine Economy	0-87083-268-9
God's New Testament Economy	0-87083-199-2
The World Situation and God's Move	0-87083-092-9
Christ vs. Religion	0-87083-010-4
The All-inclusive Christ	0-87083-020-1
Gospel Outlines	0-87083-039-2
Character	0-87083-322-7
The Secret of Experiencing Christ	0-87083-227-1
The Life and Way for the Practice of the Church Life	0-87083-785-0
The Basic Revelation in the Holy Scriptures	0-87083-105-4
The Crucial Revelation of Life in the Scriptures	0-87083-372-3
The Spirit with Our Spirit	0-87083-798-1
Christ as the Reality	0-87083-047-3
The Central Line of the Divine Revelation	0-87083-960-8
The Full Knowledge of the Word of God	0-87083-289-1
Watchman Nee—A Seer of the Divine Revelation ...	0-87083-625-0

Titles by Watchman Nee:

How to Study the Bible	0-7363-0407-X
God's Overcomers	0-7363-0433-9
The New Covenant	0-7363-0088-0
The Spiritual Man 3 volumes	0-7363-0269-7
Authority and Submission	0-7363-0185-2
The Overcoming Life	1-57593-817-0
The Glorious Church	0-87083-745-1
The Prayer Ministry of the Church	0-87083-860-1
The Breaking of the Outer Man and the Release ...	1-57593-955-X
The Mystery of Christ	1-57593-954-1
The God of Abraham, Isaac, and Jacob	0-87083-932-2
The Song of Songs	0-87083-872-5
The Gospel of God 2 volumes	1-57593-953-3
The Normal Christian Church Life	0-87083-027-9
The Character of the Lord's Worker	1-57593-322-5
The Normal Christian Faith	0-87083-748-6
Watchman Nee's Testimony	0-87083-051-1

Available at
Christian bookstores, or contact Living Stream Ministry
2431 W. La Palma Ave. • Anaheim, CA 92801
1-800-549-5164   • www.livingstream.com